A Voice in the Wilderness

A 3,000-Mile Amble over Mountains and More.

Lectures on the spirituality, physicality, and practicalities of pilgrimage.

Plus

All Aboard!
—The Last Train to Nowhere—
Rounding the Earth on earth

By

Sean Michael O'Dwyer

Author of:

A Pilgrim's Progress—Possibly
and
Hiking to Hell and Back

SEAN MICHAEL O'DWYER
THE PILGRIM OF ST. JIM

A Voice in the Wilderness

3,000 MILE AMBLE OVER MOUNTAINS AND MORE

PLUS BONUS STORY **ALL ABOARD**

Belleville, Ontario, Canada

A VOICE IN THE WILDERNESS / ALL ABOARD!
Copyright © 2010, Sean Michael O'Dwyer

All Rights Reserved. No part of this publication may be reproduced, stored in a retrieval system or transmitted in any form or by any means—electronic, mechanical, photocopy, recording or any other—except for brief quotations in printed reviews, without the prior permission of the author.

ISBN: 978-1-55452-537-9
LSI Edition: 978-1-55452-540-9

To order additional copies, visit:
www.essencebookstore.com

For more information, please contact:
Sean Michael O'Dwyer
PO Box 365
Waverly, NY 14892

Epic Press is an imprint of *Essence Publishing,* a Christian Book Publisher dedicated to furthering the work of Christ through the written word. For more information, contact:
20 Hanna Court, Belleville, Ontario, Canada K8P 5J2
Phone: 1-800-238-6376 • Fax: (613) 962-3055
E-mail: info@essence-publishing.com
Web site: www.essence-publishing.com

Printed in Canada
by
Epic Press

In gratitude
dedicated to:

Bryan and Tricia
Katy and Victoria
Dulcinea and Beatrice
St. Michael and St. Gerard
and all the other angels of God's mercy.

CONTENTS

A Voice in the Wilderness
- *Chapter 1: Entrance* 11
- *Chapter 2: Strangers and Your Cash* 17
- *Chapter 3: Beast and Beasties* 33
- *Chapter 4: The Lowdown* 53
- *Chapter 5: The Triple Threat* 61
- *Chapter 6: Something Big* 75
- *Chapter 7: The Enemy Within* 85
- *Chapter 8: Epilogue* 91
- *Chapter 9: Post Script* 99
- *Chapter 10: The Link to All Aboard* 105

All Aboard! The Last Train to Nowhere
- *Chapter 1: America* 111
- *Chapter 2: Asia* 165
- *Chapter 3: Europe* 187
- *Chapter 4: A Burst Appendix* 211

A Voice in the Wilderness

CHAPTER 1
ENTRANCE

[Enter singing Irish rebel tune]

Permit me to present: El Peregrino de Santiago (the Pilgrim of St. Jim) in full battle kit, ready this minute to march again the 3,000 miles from Florida to Canada, the long hard route over the mountains, up the Appalachian Trail. With half the gear, I will repeat doubly Europe's El Camino de Santiago (where I earned my trail name), the greatest of medieval pilgrimages, one honoring St. James the Greater, patron of pilgrims.

I have also circuited Ireland entirely, every foot on foot, and circled Earth on earth, hiking where possible: the Grand Canyon in a day; the Great Wall for a day; the Great White Way in a day (Bronx/Yonks line to the Battery by Broadway); the wind-swept steppes of Outer Mongolia; the Siberian shores of Lake Baikal. The word brought from the wide world and the narrow path:

"Be not afraid."

By this angelic injunction let all be reassured who might take up the staff of pilgrimage, i.e., any journey of distant destination or duration, bruising to the body, healing to the spirit. Most westerners, especially Americans, live in fear, are ruled by unspoken, undermining, over-riding terrors, constantly countering common sense, common decency, common feeling (all increasingly uncommon). Certainly not all these fears are unfounded, but the Bard said best: "The coward dies a thousand deaths…" if he ever lives at all. If you ever feel inspired, ACT. If you never feel inspired, die already.

Do not allow yourself to be terrorized by television, nor too entertained. Don't let the box in the corner box you in. Do not allow media sensationalizing of police or political propaganda to put you in a comfortable coffin before you're dead. If our society is sick, it can't be cured by our hiding in our houses. On the road, feet on the ground, you will confront daily the primeval forces of Good and Evil. The good news, carried from the mountains: Good wins, if you're not afraid.

No, I was not born brave. Indeed, the ill-kept journal of my recent journey begins:

2 March (or not to march) 2009

Yes, I'm scared. Having no notion of what I'm doing, I'm doing it anyway. Having since childhood said I should, I gotta try while I still can, if I can, to hike the Appalachian Trail in one season. Though only 54, I do feel old and chronically ill before starting. 55 will catch me before the Fall and the finish—maybe my finish.

Not satisfied with the daunting prospect, I'm tacking miles onto both ends. I mean to march from Florida to Canada, gulf to gulf. Having heard it can be done, I intend to do it—but I am afraid. Thousands of miles through tough topography and rough demography, all totally unknown to me, do intimidate a man lacking even gym conditioning or basic survival training. Hell, I don't even know if I want to know more before setting off.

I do know I'm scared of bears, catamounts, wild dogs and snakes, but not near as much as of diseased, infested rodents or any rabid critter. I too watched "Deliverance," and feel no desire to squeal like a pig. I own no gun, or even a bow. Let me state for the record though: I look forward to meeting folks along the way and do not believe a gun to be necessary. [Other insurance (health and life) would better serve.] However, I may be mistaken, having recently read—quite by chance—of a shocking decline, economic and social, in Florida and Georgia.

Also not anticipated eagerly is every louse, tick, spider, mosquito and fly with which Dixie famously crawls. Each in turn carries viruses, bacteria and poisonous protozoan parasites.

While we're worrying, let us not forget poisonous plants and allergenic pollens.

Above all, I am afraid of failure. If I could just accept failure, I could forego all suicidal challenges. Tomorrow's departure looms on the horizon with heavy storm clouds. Six inches of snow smothers Atlanta! A late blizzard just whomped the entire East. If I was not afeared before, I should be now.

[Author's note: This odd odyssey proved too strenuous and stressful for Ulysses to play Homer too. Journal degenerates into mere memoir here.]

Yet, I can now preach, "Be not afraid."

Let us consider what did frighten me, what might frighten you yet. First, personal weakness, possibly secret physical or psychological limitations, can paralyze. During my 3,000-mile march, every last part of my body, eyeballs to toenails, threatened to break, tried to snap my determination, destroy my pilgrimage. My first and greatest fear rose from a deep well, from my own awareness of my many weaknesses. Ergo it earns first mention; but, last overcome, it will only be touched upon for now.

Whatever was suffered, my first reassurance sprang from noting that at no time was one affliction allowed to build upon another, past all endurance. If you but ask, God does not ask more of you than you can stand. Just play your part, by behaving sensibly. God gave reason for a reason. Unlike me, start easy. Carry minimum weight necessary. I can help determine that later, but you need to start with the right attitude in your head for your body to finish the course. Banish from your mind, "I might use this; I could need that…"

There's nothing you need more than you need less!

Hike smart. Plan opportunities to hike with no pack. Devise not to do more than you need to do. For the A.T., clear your calendar for six months. El Camino requires one month minimum. Give yourself time, both beforehand and en route. Rise with the sun; sit down at sundown. Shun hectic off-trail diversions. Remember the long haul: walk, don't run; stretch, don't stress.

When trouble comes regardless (as it will), be assured: in physical suffering, spiritual healing rests.

Self-flagellation ain't suggested, but, if anyone opens himself to The Great Conscious Life Force by pulling aside daily distractions and pushing past the parameters of ordinary endurance and routine reality, the Almighty might speak to him. More than a fake wizard waits behind the curtain in Us (not Oz).

Speaking from experience, I can say what I've said, not because I'm special, but because I'm not. What happened to me can happen to you. This book is birthed to help any prospective pilgrim to attain his goal: the very voice of God. If Yahweh walks with you, *what* should you fear?

On a personal aside: I was not always a believer. In fact, I'm not a believer now. Call me a gnostic, someone with personal knowledge of The All Knowing (though uninterested in alternative gospels). Yet, most of my life I lived an agnostic. Jesuits, snaring me young, reduced my child-like faith to empirical rationalism. As I could not see, hear or touch God—a being by definition beyond human knowledge—I did not accept (or deny) His existence.

Taught pride in the power of reason, I could not make a final leap of faith. Not knowing God, I refused to jump for Him or anybody.

Christ came back for me.

Oh, I never experienced anything so dramatic as St. Paul's Damascus Road episode or Doubting Thomas's epiphany. Still, like them, I have been granted gnosis, an internal knowledge, an enlightenment by personal experience, not by reason, not by faith, not by any external info. Moreover, I can promise you, if you will align yourself entirely with life's most elemental forces, Divine Power will become evident to you. Someone close having passed-over beforehand may help, but I do not believe that necessary. So, don't be killing your brother, or he you. Let's just return to the trail now, to what might kill you there, to what you might fear. Only be aware that your journey may take you over greater obstacles than mountains. Read on. March on.

CHAPTER 2

Strangers and Your Cash

If no longer fearing yourself, you may yet fear strangers, as our culture teaches us we must. My experience on society's hard periphery schools me differently. If you try to look after yourself, total strangers will very often look out for you, happily. The whole world works like France: if you attempt to speak French, most Frenchmen gladly speak English. Decent human beings can be fashioned from most strangers if you don't estrange yourself. By being open, you allow blessings to flow, to and fro. Often strangers seek the opportunity of a passing pilgrim to become decent human beings, even in N.Y.C., especially in that city. Worry at home. Property provides a target.

On the Appalachian Trail (more than on the Pilgrimage of St. James), the above stunning metamorphosis often occurs in organized programs or serendipitously. These benefactors earn a "Trail Angel" title. A joy to meet, may joy meet them here and hereafter. Elsewhere in travels along the poverty line, I met many angels of God's mercy, offering aid and treasured memories. Hitch-hiking, frowned on by our car-consumed culture, provides many such treasures.

Hitching off the A.T. by Buchanan, Virginia, I missed likely lifts due to yet another police check. On the trooper's departure, an ex-con and moll halted their battered vehicle. Cell phone shouting further exposed cash-flow difficulties. (Piercings and tattoos-for-two pain physically and fiscally.) With no time to stow my wallet properly after the p-check, I climbed into their clunker reluctantly.

Sure enough, my wallet would work loose unnoticed when I squeezed from their compact. Two illegal u-turns by two outlaws were required to return my poor valuables. Bless 'em. Yet, how often did conveyances covered with crosses, sacred statuary and pious slogans pass me by, directly contrary to biblical edict. Drivers fail to realize the sacramentals are not talismans protecting them from their bad driving, but rather reminders to behave Christ-like. As aggressive driving harms one's health in many ways, behaving Christianly helps it. Acting like Christ includes offering lifts.

A glance should suffice to judge a man safe or insane. Drunks and lunatics you need not lift, though they are more dangerous behind a wheel, as are the sane and sober. The best you can do for yourself, your soul, your fellow man and the planet is not to drive alone. My dad could recall when no one would, long before the environment concerned any. Individualism, gone awry in America's wide-open spaces, has killed community. File it under vehicular homicide. No longer commonly socialized, we allow terror to rule. Yet, with slightest care, the chance of being accosted by anyone kindly lifted is low. Consider the great cost of not helping fellow citizens, to them and to you, then to society at large. Don't try to justify with unfounded fear your callous selfishness.

The risk certainly climbs higher for the unfortunate seeker of a free ride. Nothing is free after all. Only twice, however, in forty years of thumbing, did a lift prove worse than being left. Both times I regained the highway without bloodshed. During this most recent trip, being picked up by the Grim Reaper himself caused only momentary discomfort:

> *Before the first footfall, I needed to reach Florida's gulf coast. Surprise, no public transport connects the capital to the nearby coast. Twelve miles took three hours and three lifts, which explains my never going to that state again.*

If communal empathy has died throughout the country, the corpse has decomposed in Florida. The influx of idle bums, rich or poor, pours into the Sunshine State more than into Southern California. Hence, when Death stopped, a desperate man clambered in.

The driver, cadaverously thin and pale, introduced himself as the Grim Reaper, pointing at his scythe in the back. He further informed, he'd only stopped due to his job. Just as flight/fight alarms sounded, my Chevy Charon explained. Portraying the Reaper at a woman's 50th birthday party had been his first paid employment in many depressing months. The birthday gal and pals had so fed and fussed over him, he'd come away heartened with renewed self-esteem and good will to all. Spying me stranded, he felt compelled to help. He went out of his way.

The moral: as even the Grim Reaper can be moved to pity, you can take a lift from Death and live to tell the tale.

Truthfully, if young and attractive, or patently rich, discretion dictates avoiding either side of hitching. The rising risk factor can be cut back with little effort however. Remember, when driving, "the beautiful people" are not granted a free ride by Christ or common decency. A woman all alone does get a free pass from me, no gypsy curses. Several times lone women did stop though.

I next felt at risk when, no longer hitching, I had begun hiking back up the official trail to Tallahassee. The path passed a shack where a youth, perching on the porch, cradled a scoped rifle.

On an unseasonably warm day, he looked sorta lazy, shaded by live-oak shrouded in Spanish moss. He might have summoned the energy to shoot me, but not to drag me off the trail. I walked faster just the same, sweating more, until I reached a street sign, a sign of civilization. Unless, that is, the sign reads: "Ambush Rd." where no route crosses. Not even a driveway led to the house where a man stood watching my approach. No rifle evident, a concealed weapon looked likely as Bubba stepped down, not hiding his hostility. I walked faster still, and dreaded reaching the real boonies.

A few weeks later, the hills of Tennessee did hold me. Technically not on the A.T., I did employ official Appalachian Trail Conference (A.T.C.) charts in order to avoid their poorly planned path. Inaccuracies misled me onto private property in territory where privacy and property rights are taken deadly seriously. Landowners would not need to be moonshiners or meth dealers to feel justified in shooting at a trespasser. Run down by dogs, I could have been blasted and buried without trace. Worse, I might have been bit, beaten, shot, arrested and incarcerated legally. I escaped unscathed instead and, back on the road, was greatly aided by locals in returning to the trail.

No, I never learned my lesson. The next time I tried a "shortcut," the landowner did catch me dead to rights. More anon.

My advice, drawn from very scary experience, comes down to obtaining better maps before blazing your own trail. Expensive A.T.C. charts are kept inaccurate to hide how misleading the white blazes can be, besides to hide alternatives. Try Geographical Survey maps or even county or town-land hand-outs.

Even if you do behave yourself, the infuriating blazes can abandon a hiker entirely. "Led up the garden path" by the A.T.C., you'll need a good map then. A good guidebook, though also essential, will not suffice. Best advice? Be prepared for being lost. You will be at some point. You don't need to be flustered or fearful then. Curb feelings of frustration and betrayal, or you'll react rashly. If you've come unprepared, you had best respect religiously the white blazes, however undeserving. This author will curb himself now, reserving further comment on the Appalachian Trail Conference to another chapter.

Before attaining the A.T. trailhead, I desperately sought anywhere to walk off of asphalt. Auto traffic is easily the hardest obstacle to reaching the A.T.; its absence certainly offers the finest blessing of the trail. The second greatest danger is the stress of searching for untrafficked ways to the trailhead. One day I trespassed many miles on a path not only posted, but offering a bounty. Besides shotguns, I worried about omnipresent cell-phone or security cameras, especially when a squatting target. Escaping unharmed, maybe undetected, I passed on the next opportunity to trespass: property labeled "Quail Haven," which offered "hunting by the day," suggesting no haven for quail or me. The next shady path led only to an impressive fence and a decision to retrace my steps. When I reached the fenced property's road front, I found signs: **"Trespassers Will Be Shot."**

Shortly afterwards, another off-road shortcut led to my building a causeway through a swamp, leading only to a river and the reversing of my course, over soggier footing. Resolving then to remain on the road, I discovered the scorched-earth policy of Florida and Georgia for this Yankee. Actually, worse still, planned burning combated wild fires in March! The good news: not a cloud in the sky all week; bad news: not a cloud in the sky all week.

I was not disheartened, as God did provide a haven. Not allowing me to be shot, he led me to a Primitive Baptist Church, in the middle of nowhere, where a service thanked God for the bounty I received in the vestry (with cold bottled spring water). Later, another isolated chapel (empty) provided a shady stoop for my rest. Finally, another house of God gave shelter for my slumber (involuntarily, yet generously). More churches than homes is the rule on rural roads over much of the South. Unsure they mean success for Christ's message, I do know they all treated me well.

=== + ===

Understand, whatever transport I employed off the trail, my goal remained to cover every foot from the Florida coast to Canada on foot. I never feared the hard way, only the too stupid.

Reportedly, one thru-hiker this year did misstep into a fatal shotgun situation. A companion made a lucky escape. More good news, only one such report reached my ears. Moreover, my experience shows (much to my surprise) that the much-maligned redneck, Bible-thumping, snake-handling populace of South Georgia's rural plains must be the most decent, down-to-earth folks I ever met anywhere. Dreaded hillbilly crackers from north Georgia came a close second in genuine generosity and concern. True Christianity has not been better exhibited since biblical days. God grant help to all who offered it, especially the many proffering unsolicited (unaccepted) lifts. Though each refusal stabbed my throbbing feet, every offer did lift my heart and lighten my step.

When thirsty, I had only to knock on any door to receive bottled spring water. Offers to pay fell on deaf ears. Even walking by, looking dry, might bring from homes unsought beverages—all gratefully received regardless. Such generosity dries up mid-Georgia. Atlanta has concreted over the source.

Community, traditional rural values, shrivels in the sun. Attempts by developers, dread destroyers of community, to create and sell faux villages appear derisible, laughable but not funny. "Ye Olde Townes" mushroom around shitty cities. Old-fashioned furniture only decorates Victorian-style porches, emptied by air conditioning. Humungous houses for modern mini-families may be dwarfed by five-car garages. Forest and farmland, the wasters despoil and pave over. Truly close neighbors become distant memories. No welcome meets the stranger here, no rest for the rambler.

Good fortune found for me my cousin near Atlanta. She showed such solicitude, I left worried about her worrying. Shortly afterwards, she found cause for concern. Downtown, vicious muggers left for dead her *son*, on the floor of a parking garage. Blasted point-blank in the chest, this young man would eventually "come out of the woods" to confront and convict his attackers. Remaining in the woods all the while, I appreciated being out of the jungle.

Even in a rural county merely approaching Atlanta, where I had rung the doorbell of a roadside home, not only did I receive no water, I received no response—except a sheriff car ten minutes up the road. Ringing a doorbell now constitutes alarmingly suspicious behavior.

Having downplayed the threat from lawless outsiders, I should stipulate that fellow hikers never demonstrated real danger to me either. A rep for stealing from backpacks did shadow one shelter dweller, but I abandoned my pack for hours, hundreds of times, without regret. Accidentally, my phone and my valuables pouch were left vulnerable a few times without loss. Do beware weariness so deep that wariness slips. God's angels shielded me. Even warnings about shelters readily reached by "the general public" (code for psychopaths), I ignored with impunity.

A stout staff and a sharp knife, plus pepper spray, more than sufficed for my defense. Seldom even deployed, my weapons probably presented the greatest threat to myself. Snoring in an open shelter, I might have been bludgeoned or stabbed by a buddy, one deranged by sleep deprivation. Nevertheless, I feel the Almighty expects a certain attitude from us in return for protection: a resolve to avoid victimhood. Electing to martyr or sacrifice oneself doesn't equate with acting stupid or weak.

Only once did a situation suggest readying my defenses against a fellow grail-seeker—and that in the service of a damsel. The psycho involved, a famous thru-hiker, I met more than once. As his unsettling trail name smacked of Doomsday, let's call him "Doom."

Doom, uniquely, was recognized as crazy by people backpacking for 2,200 miles over wooded mountains for no rational notion. Our community, closely tied by shared hardship, had reason to fear Doom. First, his declared determination to hike the entire A.T. with zero funds seemed both insane and parasitic. Though a long walk in the woods might sound free, it demands about a dollar per mile in practice. The less wild Camino costs more, one euro per kilometer. Many cost savings I'll propose in these pages, but as you'll insist on making your own expensive mistakes, I strongly recommend not commencing any under-funded campaign.

However, be not afraid. Not only will I help you cut costs, many total strangers will labor freely for you, all along the way. Sometimes spontaneously, other times in organized programs, good Samaritans (on their spiritual quest) along the A.T. will come to your aid. Christians mostly, they take seriously the order to feed the hungry and care for the needy. Nobody could be needier than a thru-hiker stumbling from the woods. Your bruised and blistered body will cry unbidden to Christ for pity and T.L.C.

"Trail Angels" earn wings by offering food, accommodation, transport, medical care and hiking gear for low or no cost. Occasionally, food and drink (even booze) will be left anonymously in animal-proof containers at trailheads or shelters. If no food waits, and hikers need to hitch into town, many drivers stop religiously, despite knowing how hikers will smell. May all angels of God's mercy experience that mercy.

Though I'd like to think my body able to finish unassisted, my soul did need help on the brutal trail. "Doom" definitely required all the help he could get, and did receive enough to reach halfway at least—despite lacking any soul and hating every child of God.

You see, Doom is an alien, as he'd happily tell you. An android even, he waits for the mother ship, a battle-star, to beam up him and his ilk, before destroying the rest of us with this evil world. When first I caught up to the already dreaded doomsayer, discretion dictated pushing on to the next shelter, despite darkness descending.

Arriving late on a cold night, guided by God's grace and a campfire lit by earlier arrivals (tragically *not* typically), I felt relieved and reassured. My fellow campers were rewarded with song and story before I exhaustedly erected my tent. All headed to bed assuming I would be the last into camp. Not so.

Who had been following me through the dark forest? Doom.

He woke me by camping uncomfortably close, and again in the morning, noisily resurrecting the fire for his beloved brew-up. Still half asleep, I realized my valuables bag was missing! Fully awake, full of wrath, I unzipped the tent, only to uncover where my pouch had fallen unseen on the previous night, when I—blinded by fatigue and darkness—had tossed my pack into the tent. In morning light, my most essential stuff rested unmolested, though someone certifiably desperate and without Christian scruple viewed the easy pickings. Without love or fear of God or man, Doom turned my fear to faith in my fellowman—even in aliens. This light dawned on Easter morn.

Still, chivalry required hanging back that morning, not to leave a lady alone with a lunatic. I assumed her being more worried about an out-of-this-world weirdo than a world-wandering wildman. However, by the time her companions came into camp, I'd decided she need not have been concerned by either of us. After that, coffee was always carried for the star-man, as he craved a cuppa, for which I never cared.

Carelessness from total exhaustion must be dreaded and avoided. However weary, morning or night, number and count all belongings. The less you have, the less you can lose and live.

--- + ---

Having reassured you about the low threat level of lawless men on the trail, I should warn about lawmen off the trail. While between the white blazes, hikers hold carte blanche from the forces of law and order. Rumors run rampant about murderers and politicians wandering the woods. Past Springer Mountain, springboard of the A.T., no one has a past, not even a name. More memorable "trail names" are bestowed. However, once off the trail, a hiker reverts to hobo, preferred prey of cops. Never mind bears, "Smokey the Bear" presents the greater threat. Respect everyone wearing a funny hat, if they also sport a badge and gun. They hold you in their power. Fuhgettabout your rights. Never mind scoring points. You can win an argument and still lose big.

At all times hold upon your person two unimpeachable forms of I.D., revealing impeccable records. A clean driver's license and U.S. passport suggest a citizen of good standing—not an illegal bum. If unable to produce both, or if either indicates imperfect character, do not show the nervousness rightly felt. To further prove my not being a grifter drifter, I bore a letter from the charity for which I walked, plus another from the IRS confirming the charity's bona fides. A local newspaper article (with photo) added substance to my story. Tramping for charity seemingly means you're no insane loner, no unsympathetic figure of fun or fear. You might mention a large family or support group noting your progress, plus the book you're writing, even if you're not. Notice I wasn't lying.

No sooner dropped at Fort San Marcos by the Grim Reaper, I was reborn a "Nobo," a north-bound thru-hiker, baptized in Appalachee Bay on the Gulf of Mexico. Appalachee Indians had finished their trail there, the path for which the mountains were named, not vice versa. Of course, no self-respecting native would be caught dead on the current version. I did not know that yet. I did know that Col. Andrew Jackson had reached St. Mark's Fort in his Indian campaign. Hence my staff became "Old Hickory" headed home. The fort, after evolving into an official port of entry for U.S. immigration, remains a national park, the start of a hike/bike trail to the state capital.

How appropriate for my starting point! Yet, within 15 minutes, or one mile (of 3,000), a deputy sheriff had snagged me from the path to ask, "Quo Vadis?" and with what I.D. The A.T. was still hundreds of miles away. Taken aback, I might have let slip a cheeky response. Where was I not going? My tongue remained tightly reined, even when queried in every state, county and town from the coast to Springer, and in many towns thereafter.

Good news for the timid-hearted with wanderlust: again against stereotype, every southern sheriff and hick-town cop encountered proved professional and polite. They grew nearly apologetic about doing their duty. The full range of this vagabond's documentation may have caught off-guard his interrogators, as would requests for their names on the witness sheet for this walk. Anyone care to question the integrity of my gun-toting witnesses?

Only once would I be asked to move on. *After* I had aced the I.D. check, been told I could stay, an officer (in a famous tourist town in south Georgia) returned to reverse his decision five minutes later, even though, sitting silently in a public park, I only studied a map for the quickest way out of town. Much to his chagrin, the politic policeman explained that his captain had received another call ordering my removal. The snobby lady paid to welcome visitors convinced me she'd made the calls. I didn't match her image of the ideal well-heeled tourist. A sweaty unkempt pilgrim looked too untidy for her town, for her taste.

Oddly, I had already noted in my journal the absence of a village heart in the town, despite its fine façade. No gathering point for plain folk existed. Worse, departing town, I discovered a disturbing corruption at its center. Besides the abuse of law, I stumbled onto the old black section. Poorly lit, unpaved streets also lacked sidewalks. Though certain the welcome-center woman could provide a perfectly charming explanation, someone who had experienced her prejudice and discrimination might not be persuaded.

Just why this woman believes she owns the town, I do not know, but clearly the police agree. Their efforts, wasted on a wanderer already departing a.s.a.p., did turn a light unintentionally on a dark place. I left town pitying the policemen pushing me.

Incidentally and unfortunately, I can't complain even now about my repeated grilling. Turns out, a well-known, well-liked happy hiker (greatly benefiting from the kindness of strangers) masked a convicted sex-offender avoiding registration—until Virginia caught him.

He never represented a threat to me however.

Are you reassured yet? Well, one more word of warning then: until hitting the trailhead, you are merely a bum, favorite victim of yahoos in hotrods and raptors in cop cars. Having little choice besides trudging under pack the northbound road, a poor pilgrim presents an easy target. I did play some mad games of cat and mouse in many towns. Fortunately, cats tend to bore easily, but, you had better be carrying a couple hundred dollars, divided around your person, to beat being beaten by thieves or the vagrancy rap. Here the transcript of a recorded message from a small Georgian town should be inserted, with the proviso that I still quite like that town despite what you'll read:

> *The day finished as it began—badly. I'm whispering now, hiding in the woods at midnight, after playing hide and seek with the police for the last hour. Unsure they know they're playing, or know with whom they play, I do know they don't like losing.*
>
> *"Woods" is a word too dignified for the scrubby wasteland hiding me inside town. I'm hunkered down now, and mean to stay if the cats in this cat and mouse game haven't cheated by bringing dogs. Up near the road, a hound has been sounding for ages, damn him. Canine units are the pride and joy of southern sheriffs.*
>
> *The coppers may have spotted me dashing into these bushes when their cruiser spun around the building I'd been resting behind. Oh, how I do hate running when already limping, especially sprinting through tick-infested undergrowth after dark. Worse than ticks, sharp sticks nearly took my eyes out. God gave me two warnings, one for each eye. Not being blinded might be a miracle. My left eye may need attention in the a.m.*
>
> *I only came into town to look for a bus to Atlanta. New boots are needed before backpacking another step. In the absence of a bus, a better location for hitching would need to suffice. Hitching tried to no avail, probably too late, I resolved to try again tomorrow if the police will let me. One car I did cadge today. It carried me a whole half mile to a "better spot"—directly outside the county jail.*
>
> *I limped back to town after dark.*
>
> *If my bad leg isn't bad enough, my left hand swelled today for no reason. Pretty ugly. Reaching town, I plunged fingers*

into a cup of ice from the Subway shop. This first aid proved effective enough to remove a ring at least. Despite persistent pain and worries, I'm weary enough to sleep now, consoled by the hope that all might be better by morning. Meanwhile let's hope this recording is not taken and used in evidence."

Amazingly, everything did look improved in the morning light. I hitched to Atlanta, where R.E.I. Outfitters graciously granted a 50 percent discount. I then bused and hitched back to the above town, where I recuperated a couple days, breaking in the new boots, before marching onward.

A wee old man on his owney, I trudged 3,000 miles without real trouble from the forces of law or of lawlessness. Who remains to fear?

--- † ---

One group does remain to endanger your pilgrimage. Remember the aforementioned minor official, one paid to help tourists? Between the poles of law and lawlessness sits autocratically those who would be laws unto themselves: petty tyrants in service jobs, puffed up on their paltry power. Beware bureaucrats, bus drivers, hotel staff, shopkeepers, park rangers and—most of all—Appalachian Trail Conferees. The latter earn their own chapter. When most vulnerable, you want to trust people paid to assist the public. Don't. Insignificant though they be, they can hold enough power to wreak havoc on your plans, to cast your life completely into chaos and misery.

Pray God saves them and protects you from their plague of pettiness and presumption. My advice: don't be lulled into any false sense of security when stumbling from the deep woods. Just when ready to relax, you must stay sharp. Though your needs seem small, you need greatly. Weary as you will be, concentrate when emerging from the forest into the jungle. Do not expect pity from petty people.

When transported, you'll need to know more about local routes and schedules than do locals. At check-in and check-out counters, keep checking. Here on the real front line, you're best having company. On the A.T. or other pilgrimages, walk alone for most effect; but at day's end, sharing experience can build and enlighten it. Better, sharing expenses can lighten those and lessen loads. Hooking up along the way provides more eyes and ears to catch those who would disadvantage, discourage, dismiss or otherwise "dis" a lone hiker.

In my determination to be fast, first and self-sufficient, I foolishly failed often to pal-up. That task isn't so easy. Most hikers happen to be too much or too little like me. By being too competitive, you often lose in life.

Take special care when the A.T. snakes into a state or national park. The going will improve markedly, encouraging the naïve to pick up packs, but once away from the highway, the footing invariably deteriorates rapidly. Hiking boots soon muddied, so is the ass on which you've fallen. Muddier still, diverse regulations govern your sojourn within park boundaries. Mind-numbed nomads, dragging one numb foot ahead of another for months, must suddenly be alert to any regulation rangers have opted to enforce. A campaign of months falls subject to any official whim. Susceptibility climbs higher towards the end, peaking on the final summit, Katahdin, in Maine's Baxter Park. Baxter requires written reservation and confirmation, with pre-paid fees. Authorities accept no credit card in the park. How officials expect thru-hikers to comprehend and comply with every rule before reaching park limits, I don't understand. I do know I didn't know when I would likely find the final shelter (and ranger station) within an expansive park beyond the "100 Mile Wilderness." Heaven help you if you just show up like I did—quite innocently.

God did aid me. Though the rangers rebuked and banned me, their punishment proved providential. Having already conquered the difficult Katahdin climb, I was *almost* arrested and *was* transported to where I'd entered the park, very near the only re-supply point, and on my preferred route to Canada. You may not be so blessed though.

I never knew until nearly in the park (October 4) that it closed officially on October 15th but could be closed at anytime, quite arbitrarily (but attributed probably to bad weather). Already the mountain approach closed every day at 9:00 a.m. in October. That's nearly rightfully, as climbing Mt. Katahdin turns out to be a demanding, dawn to dusk, 9-to-5 job.

I could research and report correct procedures for entering and camping in each county, state or national park from Georgia to Maine, but that would be pointless. All rules might be altered already. This cautioning will need to suffice—with one addendum: border officials operate still more capriciously. However, as you will see, even devils can be deflected into doing divine will. Be cautious near petty tyrants, but do not be afraid.

CHAPTER 3

Beasts and Beasties!

If not afraid of man, what should you fear? Beasts? Maybe...

Let's begin this examination at the beginning, geographically and alphabetically. Alligators are the most fearsome killers from Florida to Canada, and did concern me initially. They crossed my path down in Florida, but only there, and not while I was looking. I didn't go looking for them, and they didn't look for me. Tenting along that trail to Tallahassee isn't recommended though. I certainly pushed my pins all the way to a motel. Keeping hams and calves away from gators only requires keeping your dawgs moving, away from muddy pools. If anybody lets a gator get him, the bad-ass lizard should be applauded for cleaning our gene pool.

The seriously insane, hiking Florida to Canada, like to start by wading through swamps, up to their chests in filth, alligators and water moccasins. Having already lost their minds, they don't mind being out of their heads with swamp fever, or over their heads in quicksand. Seriously, why?

"B" comes second, but bringing bears scores first for scaring me—rightfully so. Bear teeth and claws, strength and speed lend easily to legend. As a child, I roamed the wide woods without worry because hunters and loggers had blasted and blighted every bear away a century before, except from my imagination. Testifying to bruin toughness, the bruisers returned to overrun that region in Upstate N.Y. Suddenly a peaceful path might lead to sudden death.

Coincidently, shortly after, I left for Ireland (for 30 years), where no bear, no wolf, no lion lurks. Foxes do roam, but without rabies. Best of all for hikers: no snakes skulk in the shamrocks, thanks to St. Patrick. Even wild landscapes may be wandered without wondering. Deliberately returning to perambulate through the heart of "bear territory" admittedly did bother me some.

Bad news first: I experienced close encounters with at least 16 bears while playing the GA-ME (Georgia to Maine), mostly between Tennessee and Virginia. The good news: I'm here to write about them, so I will, even if the suspense is spoiled. The initial incident startled me most, since shockingly little wildlife had shown itself prior to The Great Smokies National Park.

As the first infamous hill after Fontana Dam was climbed with a 40 lb pack on my back, near Eastertide, thoughts of crucifixion weighed on my mind. Prayers from my childhood popped into my head and out of my mouth aloud. Hey, a man alone in the wild may say what he pleases; besides, I swear my load did lighten before the ridge was reached. There, the trail altered from rising zigzags to straight ridge track, a yard wide. From the path, left and right, the slope fell off sharply, leaving little choice but straight ahead—to where a bear blocked the way, ten yards away.

My first thought: "Good thing I've said my prayers. That leaves more time for screaming." Second thought: "Good thing I prayed aloud. The bear's expecting me." (Bad as being surprised by a bear might be, surprising one is worse—as I can testify.) Third thought? "Oh look, two more bears. All the best bear stories have three bears." The latecomers, clambering up the slope, looked like adolescents, big enough to do damage, but still invoking a mother's protective instinct.

Having stepped into the worst possible bear scenario, I

began walking backwards out of it, while observing how long one big cub took to walk into it. "You fat brat, your ma will kill me because you're lazy." The more obedient offspring sprang over the path and into the brush before the second showed. With a sudden lurch, his mother pushed him after the first, and plowed into the bushes last. Silence followed a brief thrashing of branches.

After waiting awhile, I sidled forward to peek over the edge. Three bears stood staring back. As the law of gravity ruled in my favor, the group turned in unison to gallop down the precipice. Then, the oddest thing happened: I started feeling sorry for bears. A little family had been frightened into a headlong downhill rush, an action bears don't do well.

Through empathy a song flowed from the heart, a sad Irish lullaby, to reassure those fleeing that I remained above on the path, not pursuing. All three bears stopped, turned, and pricked up their ears to listen. Not recalling all the words, I repeated the chorus and departed, before the critters could turn critics.

The identical song I employed again after surprising a second bruin family. Foolishly loping in the gloaming through the forests of Virginia, prime feeding time for bears, I rounded a bend to face the ass end of a bear barreling off the path. Spotting two tiny cubs, cute as buttons, sprinting ahead only soured my stomach. Five seconds sufficed for the tykes to race 20 feet to a tall tree, plus 30 feet up it, claws clicking quickly, like a zipper closing. Meanwhile Mama took covering action…

Rising on her hind legs, she wheeled to face me, claws and jaws held wide to hold me. In a brutal ballet this pirouette was repeated, for me to recount her two-inch teeth, a grand final view. Continuing along the trail more cautiously now, I softly lilted my own funeral dirge, and prayed Ma would not charge. The bear, however, impressed by my previous speed, kept her back to the bear-bearing tree. She couldn't chance my catching her cubs by outflanking her charge. Ya, right.

Still alive, I learned to respect creatures far more level-headed than canine head bangers. In confirmation, I inadvertently broke bear blockades on shelters late at night, twice. The besieged, nervous in open-sided structures, showed surprise at my unmolested arrivals. I was surprised to learn from the journal of the second shelter (Shenandoah National Park) that I had just traversed, at the trot in the twilight, the territory of eight sighted bears.

In the morning a doe shocked me by bringing twin fawns to within four feet of me in the camp clearing. On the trail I passed within reach of a deer. The peace of Eden can be slightly spoiled, however, by boldness in bucks. Deer should fear. Being worried by Bambi seems silly, though, once bears don't scare you.

Official attitudes towards bears veer towards alarmist. Wanted posters—with pictures—warn of "rogue bears." Serious fines, for failing to hang food bags ten feet up, scared me more. Despite repeated instruction, I seldom hung food far from me. In a shelter or tent, I kept provisions with me in heavy-gauge garbage bags. True, a bear can sniff out a sealed jar of peanut butter in a plastic bag left under water; but a bear hungry enough to attack would do it for the whiff of p.b. on your breath or Dorito dust on your fingers. My attitude is this: any vittles I bear over mountains will be eaten by me, not by bears (or rodents), if I have to beat the bears with a stick!

To prove the point, let me relate the third time I serenaded bears. After a long day of hard hiking, I sat playing chess, one of few games enjoyed on a set schlepped all the way. The play was interrupted by a distinct rustling and snorting in the bushes. This disturbance we dismissed as a fellow hiker's struggle to hang his food bag. Hearing the commotion repeated, I realized our man was the target not the source. My penlight grabbed from the game, I ran towards a tougher match.

Unaware of the threat, the guy holding the bag had to be pulled back to the shelter while my light played on the bushes. All strangers to me, any thru-hiker apparently could expect me to risk my life for them. I do admit being scared. Fear manufactured anger. Back at the lean-to, I picked up my stick. Hard hickory began drubbing every nearby tree and drumming the shelter beams.

Failing to summon "Come Out You Black and Tans!" I let rip with "Whiskey in the Jar." The finale finished with a flurry of stones thrown into the shrubbery. I intended to demonstrate my *not* being intimidated by any display I could out-perform. Fortunately, my audience demanded no encore. Darkness passed without incident, other than the rescued rambler's snores waking me with an *awful* start.

We never met again until Maine, where he told me of his singing away a bear in New Jersey (famous for bear). Maybe my bear back in Virginia was only a buck, but a bear not seen scares more. The most terrifying bear-I-never-saw looked for me near Damascus, Virginia, where once more I flew through the woods at twilight. (Please promise never to follow my bad example.) Off from the path a cute cub scampered squealing. I bolted in terror, my mind racing faster, "Where's Mama?"

Trusting junior to flee towards his mother, I dashed away, too late to do otherwise, and reached town in record time. Phew!

These tales are retold, not to frighten but to reassure. If I escaped mauling, you can escape unscathed. If you're not totally stupid, black bears are brainy enough to leave you alone.

Let us stress, we are discussing black bears, not grizzlies. "People" isn't listed on the menu of black bears. Grizzlies snack on their littler cousins and on just about every other creature on the continent. I'm not comfortable even contemplating those grisly murder machines. What advice besides avoidance can be offered?

Two tales about grizzlies traveled the trail:

Q: What do you do if, completely unarmed, you are charged by a grizzly?

A: Throw shit in his face. Don't worry, plenty of ammunition will be available, but you may want to practice your draw from your drawers meanwhile.

A possibly apocryphal story tells about a big b'ar found dead in a fisherman's camp in Glacier National Park. Under the brute, the rangers found the fisherman equally dead. Still in his fist, the "little cannon" had stopped the bear with only one 50 cal. round, but too late. Only one handgun (a.k.a., "the wrist-buster") could have done the job. The mystery deepened when six more holes were discovered in the carcass. An autopsy disclosed in the grisly guts another fisherman, still holding an empty 44, which could have delivered fatal indigestion eventually.

Seriously, a can of bear mace weighs pounds, a gun even more. Would an air horn help or only annoy? Plenty of backpackers set out on the A.T. packing more than packs. I began with a machete. I don't know anyone who continued "packing" past the first few mountains. Maybe I would reconsider on the Pacific Rim Trail where grizzlies hunt.

The graver problem with packing weapons would be the police. Laws vary widely between states. Personal protection could land you in a heap of trouble, maybe under a mound of earth.

The worst drawback to packing heat is its being packed precisely when needed. Keep long hickory in your hand wherever/whenever you ramble, whatever else you carry. A strong staff saved me when a savage hound sprang from nowhere, i.e. from near a house in rural New England. My wooden guardian leapt into action of its own accord, cutting the crisp fall air, striking sharply the pavement nearest snapping snarling jaws. Bowser managed to keep all his teeth by yielding the public highway to me. He might have killed me still, had any vehicle swept the curve right then.

Only when the whelp went home did I have time to draw the pepper spray. Turning back to properly season the beast did cross my mind, though his owner might have ass-salted me (shotgun loaded with rock salt), or worse. The unseen owner most deserved retribution anyhow.

My father passed down what his grandfather taught him, "Never walk-out without a stick, as you never know when you might meet a mad bull or a mean snake." Of far greater danger would be stupid people's pets, further evidence of society's decline. Don't talk to me about gun control until you can control your dogs. So precious did my staff become, when it nearly fell over a high falls, I sprang closer to the cascade to rescue a stick. I would donate it to my charity though.

The chance of meeting a bull, while rambling Amerikay today, slides into slight, due to artificial insemination and the extermination of small farms. Once the leading cause of death on farms, bulls surrendered that title to tractors. In Europe, particularly Ireland, any cross-country jaunt is far more likely to involve a bull. If you do meet a bull, remain calm. Try singing softly. If charged, swing your cudgel for an eye, while pivoting to that side. Keep up the game until you reach a tree or fence.

Very occasionally the A.T. "green tunnel" opens into wide pasture where cattle can present a problem. Though facing a bull remains unlikely, poop traps threaten not only boots but your guts. Water contamination provides the second greatest obstacle to completing pilgrimages (look out for #1). No staff, however mighty, can guard against staph, e-coli, or the dread giardia (a.k.a. "gotcha"). The appropriate response will be discussed after we've finished warning about big horns, claws and teeth.

The most dramatic threat comes from one small herd mislaid in Tennessee by nomadic African tribesmen. Actually, our government deliberately imported Watusi cattle to cut the spread of thorn brush over a grassy knoll ecosystem, unusual in the Appalachians, more typical of Ireland. Noting the six-foot horn span, I naively assumed our government had taken the obvious precaution: importing steers only.

Before directing unsuspecting defenseless ramblers through its range, the government ought to have operated on unsuspecting bullocks. First, clipping aggressiveness in bulls, and secondly the defensiveness of calving cows, the snip could also prevent unknown environmental repercussions. Turns out, no one is taking responsibility. The herd just keeps doing what comes naturally.

Assured beforehand about the exceptional docility of this fierce-appearing breed, I was afterwards told the opposite by someone who had worked with Watusi cattle locally. What's sure: the A.T.C. expects you to saunter through a wild herd of foreign cattle so tough they prefer thorn brush to grass. Cows are still cows however, not nervous-nelly high-strung horses. I glided through the gate while the cud chewers watched and listened contently to my "So-o-o, bossies."

So, of course thoroughbreds waited in the next pasture. Very territorial, they stamped and pranced. Easy, easy does the trick, but do not hesitate or retreat. I met a blue roan so beautiful I worried more about hitting her than about her hurting me.

Incidentally, in this section where Tennessee overlooks North

Carolina or vice-versa, Ireland looks over Austria! Really. I recommend this section, and many others, for section-hiking.

Not far beyond, just inside Virginia, but nearly in Scotland, the Grayson Highlands holds herds of wild ponies. Those highlands are further off than they ought to be, as the trail to there, besides being badly marked, swings weirdly wide just prior to their first shelter. Ah, once more the A.T.C. rears into this story, but, keeping it at bay with a swipe of my stilo, I return to ponies.

One small herd huddles around the stupidly distant shelter (wisely two-story). Cautious campers waken upstairs to the clatter of hooves on floorboards, plus the even more ungodly noise of horse-teeth gnawing wood. The ponies, desperate for salt, chew wherever sweaty hikers have set bums, backs, packs or hands. Elsewhere in the park, larger herds of wild ponies, unheard of in the east, can disconcert. Yet, in the end, they only provoke pity. No other point on the A.T. tempted me to interfere with Mother Nature's decidedly unmotherly nature.

Backing away from the horns of that dilemma, we return to the horns of bulls, ones you will face on the A.T. if you march as far as Maine, or maybe Vermont and New Hampshire. Of far more danger than bears, bull moose in late fall will charge a moving train or truck! Moreover, moving too near a moose, you might be blasted by an over-eager hunter.

A dozen moose crossed my trail at close range. Thousands of tracks (plus piles of scat) spake of many near misses. Only twice did bull moose confront me on the trail. The second moose was met by moonlight, an experience immediately inserted into my never-to-do-again list. The pelts of young specimens appear surprisingly dark. This particular pelt certainly surprised, materializing in the shadows ahead. My response? Repeat what worked in daylight.

Raising my stick shoulder high, I stepped forward, while rapping every trunk and rock passed. I reckoned these bulls old enough to be aware of the power in man's "magic sticks." In both cases my opponents did back off. Though they made way, they never bolted as deer do. Indeed, the largest species of deer move more like cattle, very deliberate. Both bulls seemed to deliberate deploying the horns, and decided against it—a miracle, considering what head bangers moose are.

The most unsettling experience with this species oddly didn't involve a head-on with a male. No, a retreating adolescent cow produced from me a cold sweat and a mace canister. An unseen dip in the trail ahead conspired with the odd locomotion of moose, to conjure a scary illusion.

Sensing movement ahead, I rounded a bend just in time to spy a wolf slipping away. Pointed ears visible beyond dark high shoulders, moving in a dog-trot, all suggested lobo. As my own trot slowed markedly, most of an hour hurried by before I made contact with "the wolf." This gangly heifer had been running from me all the while.

That reminds me of another spindly legged hornless creature, one much less harmless. Their reputation alone nearly killed me.

Somewhere mid-Georgia, as aforementioned, I was caught trespassing, because of a totally unexpected patrol of llamas. These foreigners, known for their territorial aggressiveness, pushed me against a herd of horses and donkeys (even more territorial). The sole avenue of escape was a maze of old fencing, leading towards a house holding a pack of hounds. Spotted by the owner, ordered to halt, I pressed on to the gate, and over it to the highway, before hounds could catch me. Full-metal jacket hounds could have caught me, had the irate landowner been prepared. An earful he did shoot at me, but not of lead. Bless him.

If I never allowed the largest or fiercest animals in the region to push me off the path, what would? Something did…

Think small. Coyotes are smaller than wolves, and more solitary. Their calls echo across the valleys in most Appalachian states, especially the more northern. A story stalked the trail about a thru-hiker savaged by coyotes which in the absence of wolves had grown larger and more social.

Only in the sparsely populated Great North Woods did this rumor pounce. By then, you'll be pushing so hard, the hounds of hell could not deter you. Off trail, domestic dogs form a far greater menace than do wild dogs anywhere.

Way back in Georgia, I rounded a bend to spy six outsized labs tear across a field—not at me, thank God. Pitying whatever poor creature they harried, I hurried my aching dawgs. Sure enough, their victim too fleet, the pooches emerged from the woods to settle on me. As I had nearly reached their owner's home, I could be entertained by laughably ineffectual calling from the porch to the pack. The limp commands were not entirely useless, however, as I learned to address the demented demons by name. Rapping the road with my scepter, I could decree, "Ginger, bad dog, go home!"

Each retriever looked perplexed at my knowing them, and at my knowing what they knew: that they were bad when in the road, ignoring their master. From wolfish, dogs turned sheepish. Of course I had crossed the road already, and timely vehicles broke up the attack. Primarily my flailing staff gave pause for thought. The owner's calls showed more concern for pets than for me. A fence would have served better.

Within an hour this scene would be replayed at another home with even more dogs and less daylight—probably the same family (people and pets). Why are such people allowed to keep pets?

Back on the trail, wild cats are worse than wild dogs if you ramble in the Rockies, but back east, the very few keep a very low profile. Wild pigs occupy a somewhat similar position.

=== + ===

Raccoons, the next size down, would be too small to cause concern were they not too clever and bold in acquiring food, your food. Skunks, still smaller, but still bolder (as we're defenseless against them), don't climb as cleverly (except the even smaller spotted skunk—very uncommon). However, both coons and skunks, even more than dogs, fall subject frequently to rabies. Since, when healthy, these species show little fear near humans, recognizing a rabid specimen can be fatally difficult. According to journal entries, I passed within days of possibly deadly attacks.

One occurred down south, where rabies seems more rampant. A Virginian shelter journal recounted an epic, two-hour running battle between three campers and one rabid skunk. The author, obviously not a country boy, failed to reckon that any mad skunk must be a rabid skunk and must be killed. Instead, when the onslaught began, he assumed having tented too near the critter's den.

Understand, if ever a skunk attacks with his teeth, you're crazy if you don't bash out his brains or, given opportunity, escape up a tree. The campers in this case kicked at the critter clawing and biting at their tent. Then they elected to decamp, along with another tenter, leaving themselves open to surprise attacks all along the trail. Not one among the three held a decent stave for staving in the skunk's skull. They fended off the fiend as best they could with silly ski poles until the beast bit one of the blokes, who, "going mad," stomped his tormentor into the dirt.

The real danger had yet to be met: microbes from the beast's saliva. Though 14 jabs by a monster needle into the belly are no longer required, treating rabies remains painful and urgent. Though necessity insisted on a night march, even these foolish unfortunates did not die, however. Indeed they are immortalized on the A.T. Confirming their legend, I had noted skunk fur scattered along the path leading to that shelter.

The raccoon attack sounded even more fearsome. Imagine you are peacefully asleep in a shelter, along with friends, all snug in your sleeping bags. In the pitch dark you're woken by jaws clamping on the base of your skull. Held by the beast and your bag, your body is able only to loose a bone-chilling scream, awaking your companions into a nightmare.

Scrambling from their bags, they try to help, while your torso whips every which way, futilely attempting to loosen a death grip. Crying out to Christ, you finally fling yourself forward, heaving the animal over your head, out of the shelter, as a piece of scalp rips free. Where he goes nobody knows, but you know you need to leave the shelter to seek medical care. Profuse bleeding from an open wound presents only your preliminary problem. No ambulance can reach you, even if one could be reached by phone.

Someone suggests a road, seven miles away, as the best bet. If the coon keeps back, you can reach the road by morning—if you don't get lost.

In this year's case, the horror story ended happily, if rabies treatments can be so described. A ranger met the victim on the trail, hailing him by name, because one of the other campers had run the opposite direction to high ground and a cellphone signal. The afflicted hiker's father, himself a doctor, was able to secure the best care quickly. Presumably, the patient was put off the trail however.

To avoid that outcome:

1. Carry a cudgel, a long stout staff.
2. Sleep together in the shelters, with heads towards the rear wall.
3. Don't hang your foodstuff above your head.

4. Keeping watch develops easily in shelters as some campers go early to bed and are early to rise.
5. If tenting, pitch camp near to shelters, and keep hatches battened. Tarped, netted hammocks provide the safer option.

--- + ---

Animals aside, the primary down side to any sort of tenting arrives every morning when you waken under rain- or dew-soaked canvas. Condensation suffices to delay or weigh down your day. That daily dilemma (what to do, what to do with a wet tent?) delivers a powerful headache. Packing away wet possibly saves time, but adds weight; and mildew or black mold ruins tents and lungs.

The big drawback of sharing shelters is the sharing. Late arrivals, loud snorers, restless rollers, and little bladders conspire to rob you of essential restorative slumber. The upside comes when you learn to sleep with an eye or ear open, sifting all the night noise for danger. Keep in mind, you likely share with 100 rodents, besides two-legged rats and the rabid raccoons, all of which should be kept away from you and your food. You might think mice cute, but they pee wherever they run, and bring lice, fleas and plague. Don't forget two-winged rats. Bats bring rabies big-time.

Another foul creature that sure scared me on the approaches to the A.T. is the common chicken. From my notes comes this entry from one day short of Springer:

> *"Chickens! The county next to Dawson Co. could easily double its property values and tax base simply by declaring itself a chicken-free zone. No breath-gagging battery farms; no tractor trailers transporting 10,000 barely live birds; no lung-collapsing loads of rotting carcasses, poop and feathers:*

how much is that worth? Amazingly, America still imports chickens from Asia!

Talk about assault and battery. Battery farms assault senses and sensibility (besides digestive and immune systems). This is early in the year; I can't imagine walking here when heat and humidity hit.

At least you know, when the air smells putrid, you're close to the A.T. trailhead. A chicken-free county could charge hikers a toll. I'd pay. Then, maybe Dawson would create an approach to the "approach trail" in Amicalola State Park. How about a path away from the chicken-trafficked roads?

Only one vehicle hit me harder than the monstrously fowl trucks: a yellow cab. No, I wasn't run down by a wayward taxi. A fellow hiker, "less driven" than I, had hired a hack, from Dawsonville to the park. Starting trail camaraderie early, he stopped along the way for me. Of course I couldn't accept, but learned I had nine miles to go. About a mile later for me, the cabbie came back, beeping as he passed, without a notion of how much that honk hurt or the last eight miles would drag.

Psychological pain aside, I suffered physically by the time I attained the first A.T. shelter, just inside the state park. Seeking ice and aspirin to lessen the swelling in my legs is how I finished my day and began the Appalachian Trail.

P.S.: As much as the hiker with the hack hurt me unwittingly, I meant to thank him properly when I finally caught-up. Pretty confident about catching him, I was convinced I could pat his back without hitting him from behind. Passing him proved even easier than expected. He had turned back by the second day, due to the beating given his knees by the brutal trail. I never wished that on him, I swear. The fella struck me as truly genuine.

P.P.S.: Beware of wild poultry. An explosion of quail can quail you; a game hen, more than game, is a frightful drama queen.

≡≡≡ + ≡≡≡

Okay, don't say you've not been warned now, not after that page from my diary of disaster. Technically, I wasn't chicken of chickens however. When I held my breath and closed my eyes while hoofing clear across a county, I was more concerned with pestilence, which brings us to the scariest, teensiest demon on the A.T., the deertick nymph, carrier of the terribly debilitating Lyme disease. No defense protects against this spawn of Satan.

"Heresy!" I hear you say. I don't care; I contend the devil created these specks of evil. Blood-sucking black flies and mosquitoes probably afflict the flesh more, but psychologically the ever-lurking ticks, the ever-looming Lyme disease torments more. Undetected, these insidious insects ambush you in the long grass, or stealthily lay-in-wait on long leafy tendrils, or ninja jump from overhead branches. For God's sake, keep on a big hat and long pants. That's the least you can do, before asking for God's help, and unfortunately, about the most you can do. You can dowse clothes or person in pesticides besides, but I suspect that's only something more for the invincible ticks to bury under your skin. Some areas ought not to be entered in certain seasons or weather.

The disease they carry first manifests itself with muscle fatigue and joint pain. Who on the A.T. doesn't suffer from these? A bull's-eye rash developing around the bite also indicates Lyme. However, most hikers develop widespread rashes, and only most victims get the tell-tale bull's-eye.

By the time any symptom is noted, you're likely too late to fully avoid long-term wasting effects. Heavy dosing of Doxycycline, the only cure, produces side effects of muscle fatigue and joint pain, plus a wasting of body tissue. That's enough to make anyone hesitate, at least until he's sure about having contracted the disease, spread only by half of deerticks, a fraction of all ticks.

Moreover, you can save yourself by finding and removing ticks (entirely) if in time. No test provides a sure result though. Common false positives and false negatives make for disconcerting uncertainty. You can be certain results will take longer than necessary. Your tri-combo of antibiotic gang busters will defend too late if you wait until you know you need it.

The most diabolic aspect of this devilish disease must be the unexpectedness of the onslaught. In each case the tick anesthetizes the victim before biting, after underhandedly climbing to some secret unseen place. Worse, when I was young, the entire epidemic was unknown. We all walked without worry through the woods. When first noted in Lyme, Connecticut, the pestilence was presumed a southern swamp fever migrating north due to global warming. No such scourge existed in the South though.

Yes, ticks (large buggers) do prevail below the Mason-Dixon Line, biting me 16 times from Florida to West Virginia. At least 40 more I caught on clothes and bags before they bit. Like battalions of special forces, these legions of Lucifer attack the lone hiker from every direction. Only the final wee fecker in West Virginia looked like a deertick nymph, i.e., damn near invisible. At the Harper's Ferry (West Va.) H.Q. of the A.T., a map displayed the worst concentrations of Lyme disease: Eastern Pa. and N.Y., N.J., R.I., Mass., Vt. and Conn. (not Dixie at all). I fear this plague might be something new and man made. Man certainly seems to be doing little to stop it. The A.T.C. particularly should be doing more, warning more at least, and redirecting. God showed me that map. Every second person on the trail told of experiencing this debilitating disease directly or indirectly with a dear one.

No tick, I found, found me above Dixie, though '09 was

declared a bad tick year. My own large-scale evasive action deserves credit (not the A.T.C.)—more on that in the next chapter.

For now, let this suffice: I elected to avoid the black heart of pestilent territory by blazing my own unbroken trail entirely around the area of highest infestation. I feared not the deertick however, so much as I feared God. As He had preserved me miraculously to date, deliberately turning towards Hades looked like spitting in the face of the Father.

Canada bound, I resented already dipping south and east after Duncannon, Pennsylvania, just to trip the reputedly roughest trail on the A.T.: the awfully and awesomely named "Ankle-buster." As I marched for a charitable cause (a cure for Parkinson's), risking sponsorship by deliberately taking a diabolically misdirected route smacked not only of irresponsibility but of the confessional.

Moreover, a huge, hugely significant family gathering was due to open, due north, directly up the Mid-State Trail. By adding the Fingerlakes and Erie Canal trails, I could work my way around to Massachusetts by September when tick activity dies down. Not intending for the Ankle-buster to beat me, I could return to complete it later. We'll return to that later, later in this book.

Besides, as the sole clear break in the Appalachian chain, the Mohawk Valley warrants the attention of A.T. hikers. Dramatic scenery and history wait for the wanderer there. Derelict factory after factory stand as stark memorials to our prosperous industrial past, or as monuments to our monumental stupidity and current decline. Ilion, N.Y., provides the exception: the Remington works. The oldest gun manufacturer in America continues to flourish. Any commentary necessary?

An interesting free museum is on offer. How's that for a positive comment?

While bear and moose should not frighten you from the trail, concern over smaller creatures should not be limited to the woods. The most dangerous animal in the world is the dog next door. Other wild critters lurk around the corner too. The worst bite I received on the A.T. could have caught anyone anywhere. A sweat-bee nipped me without my even knowing.

I only surmised the assault after my eyes began swelling shut. Backpacking blindly into the "100 Mile Wilderness," when literally going blind, and possibly breathless, does look risky. Yet, an allergic reaction at work, or while driving home, would be worse. Someone did offer to drive me to a clinic, but I just borrowed ice, and barreled on.

The state of Maine is big and bad enough to be the State of Despair for any thru-hiker, nobo or sobo. Way back in flat Florida, my resolve was sapped by high heat and heavy pack. Thank God I never started from Springer, never mind from Katahdin. Statistics state that a nobo holds a better chance of completion than a sobo. Before Springer, mid-Georgia, I hit "Colquitt County" and counted this blessing: Colquitt hadn't tempted me before. If I didn't call quits in Florida, I couldn't in Georgia; and no way would I in Maine—not for a wee bee, not for a nest of hornets.

A nest of vipers might have done the trick. Snakes prefer warmer climes though. Many notices warn of snakes along the way, and caution against killing them, but rattlers provide warning themselves. I came to appreciate these genteel reptiles, over more aggressive, silent killers like copperheads or moccasins. The snake seen most, however, the blacksnake, often found sunning on the path, kills other snakes. All snakes kill rodents, probably the greater threat to you. I vote for a blacksnake to be left in every shelter. Back home, anyone might find a rattler in their house or barn.

Inside my own home, I received the worst bite of all. A spider, regarding me (after long absence) as an intruder, gnashed my leg nastily. As the seeping wound wouldn't heal, I suspected a brown reclusive might be the culprit. These new sneaky migrants to my region could cost a man an arm or a leg literally. No salve helped except for veterinarian bag-balm for cattle. That did the job.

A poorer outcome (heard on the A.T.) occurred for a housewife who contracted Lyme without ever leaving home. Her hunter husband never caught it, but carried it to her in his hunting gear. His duds waylaid his missus in the laundry room. She never knew what hit her, until too late.

On a break at home, strolling through residential streets after dark, I was warned about urban blight, just before being accosted—by an eight-point buck! We only startled each other. On a suburban avenue I met a man afraid to stroll down his own street due to loose mutts and rabid raccoons or skunks. He coveted my cudgel. That stick is useless, however, against a healthy skunk, like the one living on my own street.

On the above suburban avenue I came closest to being killed, by a teenager cycling without lights on a dark night. Free-wheeling down the shoulder of a steep, sweeping curve of highway, he never noticed me, as he busily texted. At the last moment he swerved away into the road. Had oncoming traffic been any closer, we would all have been involved in a doubly fatal accident. Looks like we need a new word for stupid. "Superstuportextorous?"

The lesson: as the devil can find you anywhere, fear God, and nothing more on earth.

CHAPTER 4

The Lowdown

Ah, what about earth itself? As cleanliness is next to godliness, dirt can be diabolical. Having grown-up on a farm, used to sweating in filthy clothes day after day, I did not expect trouble from a lengthy pilgrimage. Accustomed to tramping the streets of two continents, I merely smiled and shrugged, perhaps dismissively, when a black teenage girl working at a McDonald's in Florida asked how I could keep clean. Hadn't I just abused their restroom? However, she had put her finger precisely on the largest obstacle (and the lowliest) to completing the A.T.: dirt.

Any long hike requires a plan of campaign for maintaining hygiene, because:

- You are going to sweat like never before, leaving bacteria and toxins all over your body. Marching into the unknown, you won't find showers or washers readily available affordably.
- Enough clean clothes cannot be carried; garments cannot be washed and dried often enough.
- Cotton clothes, ideal for hiking if your pack includes washer and dryer, won't do otherwise. Man made materials, essential for trekking because they do dry, induce sweat and hold odor.
- At day's end, exhaustion can drop you fully dressed into your sleeping bag, precluding any inconvenient effort at hygiene.

- Convenience, caution, modesty and time constraints all conspire to keep you in dirty clothes.
- When trekking, staying dry and warm generally trumps getting wet and clean.

Due to the above, a life-threatening danger develops quickly, actually grows on you. Ordinary omnipresent bacteria, rearing rampant on our bodies, renders every nick, nip, scrape, scratch, rash, pimple or pack sore into a serious wound. An angry staph infection calls for hospitalization and courses of antibiotics (internal and topical) in clinically clean conditions.

Not going septic in a hospital would be lucky. On the trail you're up the proverbial creek. Merely the rubbing of an ill-fitted boot can cause a leg to swell or a foot to smell of putrid flesh. What's the usual response in the woods to shit-scary?...Nothin'. Pushing on, the hiker puts on a brave face, a mask over unsettling uncertainty.

The proper "response" is pre-emptive strikes. Planning and prevention, a hygiene campaign, costs money and more, however. You need to invest time and effort. Weekly visits to a hotel (with self-service laundry) are no luxury. This necessity can be made less expensive by connecting up with fellow hikers, hopefully a positive experience. Necessity does indeed make strange bedfellows though.

Some motels cater to hikers, offering hostel rates even. Several famous hostels along the route should be added, but generally proffer far from hotel standards. Aiming more for funky or folksy, hostels don't always hit that target either. The average motel provides the best value, if you can connect with others. Hitting a good hostel at day's end, or keeping pace with like-minded hikers right into a motel, requires careful planning and diplomacy, typically past the capacity of the weary.

Worth special effort and speed, even deliberate delay, check out checking in at the following:

1. Neel's Gap, before noon, when the trail angels fly there. Find Goose Pond Camp nearby.
2. The Blueberry Patch Hostel, Hiawassee, Georgia (very friendly town; with an all-you-can-eat; good motel).
3. Elmer's, Hot Springs, North Carolina—more retreat house than hostel, in an idyllic village.
4. Kincora Hostel, Hampton, Tennessee—legendary but not purpose designed.
5. Gatlinburg, Tennessee, a entire town for R&R. No hostel, but plenty of deal-making motels. Connected by bus to Pigeon Forge: Dollywood Park, more motels and a Golden Corral!
6. Damascus, Virginia, for "Trail Days" (Daze?) in the middle of May. Meals and healthcare for free!
7. Grace Episcopal Church hostel, Waynesboro, Virginia—perfect but ephemeral.
8. Doyle's Pub, Duncannon, Pennsylvania, reunion H.Q. of the A.T.
9. Jackman, Maine—in-town campsite and laundromat. Blessed.
10. Shaw's, Monsoon, Maine—last-chance hostel before the 100 Mile Wilderness.

I could and should list more, if the effort was worthwhile, but any hiker will still need an up-to-date annual guide, which will still be out of date. Moreover, management and staff change with the wind, and though I enjoy simple living, you may be put off by primitive conditions on a bad day (for you or the facility). Ideally, any hostel should provide quiet dorms, far from cooking and social areas. Cost and cleanliness come first though.

As *your* cleanliness must concern you most, clean hot showers need to be *the* prerequisite never sacrificed. On failing to find or afford clean accommodation, employ your stock of hand cleaner, wet wipes, alcohol swabs and filtered water.

     === + ===

  Filtering water for drinking constitutes the second front in the fight against dirt and disease. For my defense I selected the best filter on the market: the Swiss-made Katadyn Vario. Apparently, the apparatus lived up to its task. Its strength furnishes its weakness however. The additional ceramic filter renders the device extra effective and extra expensive, bulky, heavy and slow. That second filter was scarcely used, as I was ever harried or hurried by thirst or the threat of darkness. My problem partly derived from my own selectivity with sources. Clear water watched bubbling from stony ground represented my preferred source. A little crystalline trickle within a tiny, visible watershed would do. Many pristine mountain streams were ruined for me by the nightmare vision of a carcass or sewer pipe around the bend upstream. I did see a delicate doe pissing in one stream.

  Old-fashioned iodine pills and bleach, while also effective, work slower, and leave a chemical taste. Chemical treatment is available without the latter drawback, but I remain uncertain about that "improvement." UV pens supposedly work, weigh far less than any filter, and don't affect taste. Taste is not always tasty though. Besides slowness, the main drawback of all filter alternatives for a thirsty man is the remaining metallic taste and residue, not to mention actual gritty bits.

  Incidentally, one tends with treatment to collect and carry too much weighty water. I remain in the market for smaller, lighter, cheaper filters. Any advice for me? I'll pass it on.

     === + ===

  Unfortunately, hikers cannot filter their food. Unrefrigerated supplies, kept and consumed in unsanitary conditions on the trail, did concern me. That turned out not to be the problem. The foods suggested below do not require refrigeration or careful handling. Our immune systems grow capable of handling most regular contamination. Botulism and e-coli lurk off trail, where the unwary assume foods have been refrigerated properly. The worst culprit could be yogurt. Missing it in the woods, I would search for bio-yogurt in town. Beware. This warning applies to everybody living in the sunbelt, not just hikers. Even national supermarkets can't seem to keep dairy products properly chilled wherever temps hit 100°F regularly.

Three times yogurt cut through my guts. The last time I thought would be *the* last time. Three strikes, you're *out* in America. The experience extended my knowledge of what the human body can spew and still survive. You could say I was "pleasantly surprised," but I wouldn't. The yogurt difficulty only indicates a general decline in food care in America. Alone in the woods is not when you need to worry. Our careless "civilization" can kill you.

Let me insert here another item on the "Never Again List." Never go on the run when you have the runs. Nobody should need "to use the bushes" when he's hiding in them. That still beats shitting your pants, inside your tent…No, but I never came closer. Mercy, mercy, mercy.

The predominant, yet most insidious, danger presented by diarrhea, i.e. dehydration, ironically can result from drinking liquids. First, you obviously can drink bad water, or insufficient good water (leading to constipation initially). An earlier sign, a headache, may even precede thirst. Curing this headache may prove a bigger headache than expected. You better concentrate on this, the hardest problem of pilgrims, because other niggling pains and injury will follow sharply.

Under heavy pack, over hard terrain, not even under a hot sun, you will perspire far more moisture than you are able to replace.

Even steadily supplied, your body cannot absorb moisture as fast as it loses it. Essential minerals, electrolytes, won't be replaced either, even if you buy and carry "healthy energy drinks." Beverages containing caffeine, alcohol or other irritants only aid dehydration. Your system also requires large quantities of water to properly digest food ordinarily. On the trail your diet, doubly dry and salty, doubles in quantity too—but not quality.

I don't recommend packing more than two liters of H20 regardless. Water, cumbersome and heavy, can make you sweat. That said, you'd best take care planning your re-supply.

The Pacific Rim or Continental-Divide Trails require serious study and contingency plans. However, the A.T. might be trickier. As you're not crossing any desert, or uninhabited wasteland, you don't expect a drought, exactly what you often find. Trust me, up on the ridges, don't trust to luck when looking for trustworthy water sources. Even sources listed in essential guides regularly disappoint. If flowing cleanly, they can be hard to locate, more distant than indicated or desired. Hiking extra miles on poorer paths, down and up steep inclines, appears patently counterproductive to a thirsty man.

The A.T.C. takes pride in directing hikers away from municipal water supplies or shops. Moreover, in a world ruled by Walmart, most villages and many large towns lack any shop less than 10 or 20 miles away, down near an interstate. Even a few miles in a wrong direction means double the distance back to the trail. Of course I don't expect consideration from international corporations, but from an organization for hikers…?

Speaking of consideration, if, living in one of the above towns, you ever hear hoarsely whispered by a gaunt figure, "Is a shop open near here?" don't answer with a question. "What kind of shop?" or "How far is near?" won't do. If I wanted Macy's or Bloomingdale's, I would've specified. An emaciated backpacker probably doesn't need an auto-repair or tanning shop. If no shop of any sort has operated for decades in your hamlet, does the sort of shop I seek matter?

If you could use a few things yourself, you could offer to drive over and back, if the store stands more than a mile off the trail. If it's more than 10 miles, you're okay, fuhgettaboutit, but spare us the stupid questions. Any building open to the public probably possesses something useful to someone with nothing. A restroom, drinking fountain, air conditioning or a bench can restore life. If you won't offer a lift, can't you give free info? Don't make us drag it out of you before we collapse.

For hikers hurting through dehydration or collapsing, I do *not* recommend pain-blockers. Pain is your friend, alerting you to bigger trouble approaching. Before pain strikes, take low-dose aspirin to combat the effects of dehydration. By thinning blood, lowering blood pressure, bringing down swelling and inflammation, buffered aspirin prevents further injury—unless you overdose.

As noted, I began the A.T. (in Amicolala State Park) looking for aspirin and ice to reduce the swelling in already damaged legs. Just a few thousand miles to go! Funny as this seems now, I was not laughing then. Learn from my suffering to suffer less.

=== + ===

Here is the most important lesson I learned. Each time I thought I might not be able to go on, I would self-massage and self-medicate (only aspirin) to spur circulation; then, summoning all of my God-given adrenalin, I would call upon Christ's holy name. Every time, help came.

To deal with general weariness or sudden danger, invoke the power of the saints. If you but choose, you are part of the Mystical Body of Christ, as are all your near and dear who died in Him. That's official church teaching and my personal experience. The communion of saints has in St. Michael a mighty smiting arm. Of course your own body will betray you, time and again, but will also heal miraculously, given the chance. Ask in Christ's name; strength and healing will come.

═══ ✝ ═══

CHAPTER 5

The Triple Threat

You may imagine that everything large and little which might kill you in the wild has now been covered and discounted. Nope, three deadly enemies, daily attackers, must still be named: your own pack, provisions and pride.

No hiker has a greater foe than the pack on his back. Your pack will powerfully ally itself with all other forces against you. Henceforth, let *"Less!"* be the battle cry when packing. Remember the backpacker motto: *"More than anything, less is needed."*

Walking 3,000 miles requires the following, and no more.

I wore or packed in two small, easily accessible pouches:

1. One stout staff (five foot minimum)—corded
2. Light, big-brimmed hat (with drawstring)
3. Running shoes
4. Three H20 bottles, two liters total
5. Wallet (well-weeded)
6. Field-jacket liner
7. Quality poncho, and carrier bag
8. Passport, license, charity ID
9. Tickets, itinerary, maps
10. Guidebooks/phrasebooks
11. Address and date books
12. Phone and charger

Note: Leave nothing in pants pockets. Don't make me list the troubles you'd make for yourself.

1. Talisman and Testament
2. Sharp knife, 12 plastic spoons.
3. Two LED flashlights, three extra batteries
4. Lighter and matches
5. Small mace canister
6. Tissues (four packets), some paper towels
7. Alcohol swabs, hand sanitizer, moist wipes
8. Stationery and stamps (plus puzzle book)
9. Mini voice recorder
10. Small filmless camera
11. Newspaper and magazine
12. Reading/magnifying glasses
13. Mini first-aid/sewing kits
14. Two heavy-gauge garbage bags
15. Duct tape (not full roll)
17. Vitamins and aspirin (low-dose)
16. Two snack-bars and sugarless gum.
18. Long-sleeve shirt; short pants

Pouches must be rigged not to cross the left shoulder, to avoid serious trouble. Use ziplock bags.

Into the backpack or onto your back goes:
1. Light hiking boots
2. Light sleeping bag
3. Tarp; very light rope (25 ft.)
4. Water filter
5. Quality pack cover (don't skimp)
6. Netted hammock or tent
7. Essential travel toiletries
8. Two very small towels
9. Flip-flops
10. Vinyl seat cushion

All of the above list could and should be left behind or sent ahead for a day or two if opportunities arise, along with most of the next list. Your total load should not exceed one washing-machine load. Avoid red gear to avoid pink underwear. The blessed Camino requires no camping gear (save a very light sleeping-bag and tarp) as inexpensive hostels for pilgrims cover the route. (reference: *Hikin' to Hell 'n' Back*)

1. 5 underpants
2. 4 T-shirts (not all cotton)
3. 5 pairs of socks
4. 3 light pants (not jeans, twit)
5. 1 fleece vest
6. Gloves (warm, light, sturdy)
7. Blanket (small and light)
8. 1 meal of non-perishables
9. Extra toiletries and first-aid
10. Future maps and guides

One of each should be posted from Atlanta (en route to Florida) to Hiawassee, Georgia, and forwarded again as convenient. *Warning:* You will likely need the warm gear in the mountains past Hiawassee, but once your parcel is open, you need to pay again to post. Pick any nearby post-office, for low postage; then call to push it to one more convenient to your itinerary. (See below: **) Your hotel in Atlanta might hold some gear while you hike from Florida. Be prepared to plead.

PROVISIONS
1. Cocktail loaf of rye bread
2. Crunchy peanut butter (16 oz. max.)
3. Two flat pkt. of tuna
4. 8 oz. block of hard cheese
5. Granola bars/oat cookies
6. Lara Bars (best fruit & nut bars)
7. Trail mix (no peanuts)
8 Corn chips (plain)
9. Chocolate
10. Chocolate covered or centered.

Look for hard bread and all-natural p.b. You may think you don't like p.b., but wait till you're on the trail. Your taste and needs will change. I started eating the stuff during the great (fatal) contamination scandal in Georgia. Your biggest craving will be for p.b. in a light *plastic* jar. All of this list will need to be slung from your pack artfully in a reusable shopping bag until supplies can be squeezed into pack or pouch.

**The best tip (touched on above) for any backpacker: the U.S. government will help carry your pack. Who expected that? For around $5.00 anybody can priority mail five pounds of non-perishables to any nearby post office; then, merely request (even by phone) for that package to be bounced up your route—for no additional charge! This process you freely repeat until you need to open the box.

Not even all post office workers know about this obvious anomaly, which even this libertarian could not wish corrected. Spain also provides a great postal deal to Santiago de Compostella, but even that notoriously profligate government can't beat Uncle Sam inside the U.S.

Address the priority-mail box (also free) to:
John Q. Public
General Delivery   [Hold for thru-hiker]

Be aware, big towns can hold more than one post office. General Delivery will be located in the less convenient one. Even more inconvenient will be the P.O. being closed whenever you hit town, probably for a long weekend. Lobbies generally remain open, another blessing for hobos.

Lastly, allow yourself one small luxury item. I carried a chess set the length of the trail, but I am a little crazy about chess. My insanity would not suffice to make me do that again. If not into luxury, a corrugated cardboard box can be acquired en route by those who can't afford an expensive self-inflating poly-cell mattress (wasted in a hammock). An even more essential item you need *not* pre-pack is a newspaper. This old trick of hobos provides emergency insulation and toilet paper, besides disposable reading material. *Most importantly*, raveled newspaper inserted in wet hiking shoes will not only dry but deodorize. If you can't afford (in cash or weight) a tent or hammock, two tarp-tent ideas will be useful. (1) Tie tarp over picnic table. Hey, presto, a tent with shelving! (2) Bend two saplings (six feet apart), tie down, throw tarp over.

Near civilization, innumerable alternatives to carrying, pitching and drying a tent are available, if trespassing fines can be avoided. Jail is one alternative not suggested. No vagrant can afford either too much or too little respect for property. Respect for the person must take priority over property. As long as I don't stay or damage property, I figure urgent personal need exceeds legal niceties. "This land is your land, this land is my land!" as Woody Guthrie sang. My rule: avoid affronting landowners or policemen by flagrant trespass in front of them or security cameras.

More thought should be given here to provisioning, because more thought will be given to vittles on the trail than to any other subject. The way to grant them less thought, then, is to consider them more now. Re-supply along El Camino de Santiago rarely supplies any problem, other than the inconvenient opening hours of shops, restaurants and hostels. Along the A.T. or other even more wilderness-bound trails, running short of food can cause serious concern. However, the first and greatest danger on any trek remains loading down your pack with too much. Both bearing too much or too little can cause fatal consequences. Let the following advice guide you.

1. Nowhere on the A.T. will you need more than three days' provisions. Even in Maine's "100 Mile Wilderness," food can be found—more than nuts and berries.
2. Your re-up should be planned so you never approach, with more than a day's ration, any store, or arrive with less than one meal.
3. As packaging and pricing forces purchases of larger quantities, try to shop with other hikers.
4. Preferably provision in towns possessing "all-you-can-eat" eateries. Golden Corral is the best, most consistent, chain. Some genuine family-run family-style dining can still be found.
5. All normal nutritional wisdom gets lost in the woods. Long treks require higher fat, salt and sugar intake. I drew the line at high fructose corn syrup, but could not escape it. Wheat, put into everything, bedevils me more. Most food intolerances disappear on the trail though. Your body burns all on a high heat, even a half-gallon of ice cream at the half way point. Don't fear that bogus challenge either (I won two wooden spoons on one day) but don't do chocolate.

Proper trail staples I have already listed. Fresh fruit and juice or canned goods can be bought and consumed in town. Do not carry that stuff on the trail, especially not in glass jars. You will be amazed where pizza can be delivered, but don't count on it. Aside from restaurants, most supermarkets and mini-markets serve hot food; hotels and hostels provide basic cooking facilities.

Having completed the entire trail "cold," I don't recommend carrying cooking stoves, fuel and utensils. Less is best. Time and energy squandered unpacking and packing pots for pottering with dehydrated, unappetizing, costly cuisine astounded me. If the camp chefs never headed into town to eat out, I could respect their judgment. Looking for canned fuel only gave them another reason to leave the trail. In town they ate with the rest of us.

Back on the trail, hot food only means fussing when you should be resting or running. You may need to run from the critters that cooking aromas attract. To those who whine, "I need my coffee," I reply, "No, you don't. Now's the perfect time to lose bad, unnatural habits, along with a little weight off your belly and your backpack."

What's with all the smoking in the woods? Hiking to health doesn't suggest smoking cigs. Dope is even dopier in the great outdoors even if narcs are entirely absent. What about forest fires? Keep matches and lighter for campfires only. Birch bark makes the best fire-starter.

As important as what you pack is the pack itself. I opted for a cheaper model, and paid dearly for that. The metal braces snapped without warning at the worst time. Kudos to Jansport for replacing the pack when it wasn't needed anymore. More kudos to the fellow hiker who helped splint the braces until they could be truly fixed by the Osprey Co.(for free) at the Damascus festival. Ensure the pack fits when its full (and you're empty). Straps should ride an inch off your shoulders.

The other essential of which too much can easily be packed is pride. Pride does put you on the trail, and pushes when you are slowed by having no food or water, no energy or light, no belief or hope. When the whole world holds only weariness and pain, pride can push body and spirit through to your goal. Yet, know pride can push too hard. Pride can cripple and derange. Pride can spoil holy pilgrimage. Beware the power of pride, original sin of Satan and of man.

Pride took for me the disarming form of a game. This little competition first appears in a little note from mid-Georgia.

> *27/03/09*
>
> *To walk from Griffin to Atlanta in a day, in this heat, under-pack, would kill most Americans, especially if over 50. Right up routes 7 and 3, Jonesboro stretches over much of the distance. Clayton County Justice Center impresses first. Simple justice requires quite the complex in this county. The Law's reaching expansiveness encouraged me to pick up the pace until passing different complexes. One after another, shopping malls and food courts competed for my attention. Here an odd experience occurred, the odder for being odd at all. A pedestrian passed me.*
>
> *For the first time in a month of hiking hundreds of miles, I experienced another person walking beside me. Shock slowed me for a second. Someone somewhere in America was actually walking from one mall to another. Since I was backpacking to Canada, I should have just let him pass. However, as that teenager's pants were nearly around his knees, I felt the need to demonstrate a proper stride. The saddest aspect of this incident is not my pathetic pride, but having had only one opportunity to display it. No wonder Americans grow monstrously fat.*

Once past Springer, I had plenty of opportunity to play the pride game. Hundreds of hikers, all headed north, comparatively crowded the trail's early stretches. In the first few states, I could dust dozens of backpackers per day, scores even. No one passed me permanently. Only after serious distance and terrain had weeded the weak from the chase did I begin to find difficulties. For sure I met my match many times around the midway point, but still always won the game, as the rules were mine and the opposition unaware. "Gutsy" I honor by name as she lived up to it, and also kindly aided me twice. She knows I earned my second trail name, "The Mad Quick Mick."

Honor requires I acknowledge the superiority of one "competitor." With an easy athleticism, a young man called "Wispee" glided by me effortlessly as we approached Pennsylvania. Never seen to run or over-exert himself, he powered past my reach in a couple days. Assuming he made his way to Maine, his way provides the paradigm. He told me how the trail saddled him with that name, but I prefer to say he earned it by passing me to disappear like a will-of-the-wisp.

I'm ashamed to say nobody else would, not all the way to Canada, not even day hikers or dog walkers. That indicates a failure to stay tuned to my own body's natural pace. The vibes of nature around me could not have been fully appreciated either. I did not allow others to dictate my pace. Pride pushed me. I'm still convinced I needed some pushing though.

The following entry in my shamefully kept diary relates how pride can help or hurt you. From 26/03/09:

> *Feeling slightly feverish from fighting pain and infection, from injury and bug bites, I do detect improvement today, but yearn for proper bed rest. The essential lesson learned: never carry more than the essential, and distribute that weight*

evenly. Even when pride declares you can handle more pounds, don't listen.

Maybe you can lift the heavier load easily. Maybe you can carry it all day without sweating. If you shoulder that load a week, every ounce will weaken you every day. Bearing extra weight, you only need to set wrong one foot once, to regret right away each unnecessary ounce. You could be sorry the next day, and maybe for the rest of your life. Try not to overdo unduly. Stress kills, body and soul. God gave you reason. Be reasonable. If, due to unforeseen circumstances, you face a forced march, call upon the power of God for help. You are not God. Replace pride with prayer. God will allow you to do divine deeds. If not, if you fail to attain your target, The All Seeing may have a reason. See if you can divine that. Then, take pride in being prepared to camp anywhere anyway.

Okay, your pack is complete. That's all you need to carry—except for one thing. Only a fool leaves behind the final prerequisite. It weighs nothing, no matter how much you bring, and it can bring you, even when you have run out of provisions, pride or prayers. Three thousand miles over mountains is far too far to go without songs.

Let loose from my lungs, or hummed to my heart, a good song lifted my feet from start to finish (as film footage shows on Katahdin). An Irish rebel tune, about the 1798 United Irishmen Rebellion, "Kelly, the Boy from Killan," most buoyed my heart and the spirits of glum and grumpy campers. Shocking to say, I alone sang along the road or around the campfires.

People, people, people, have you no songs of the people, by the people, for the people? Has our pop culture reduced us to this? iPods in ears, no lilt lifts your heart to your head. Nor am I a great singer, silencing others by my virtuosity. The opposite. My Da, who could not sing a lick, taught me to sing a good song regardless. My Father-in-heaven (both of them) saw to my being rewarded for my songs along the road, or allowed me to reward all who gave freely of themselves.

Kelly, the Boy from Killan

What's the news? What's the news, oh my bold Shelmalier,
With your long-barreled gun from the sea?
Say what wind from the south blows its messenger here,
With a hymn for the dawn of the free.

Goodly news, goodly news, do I bring youth of Forth,
Goodly news shall you hear Bargey man.
For, the boys march at morn, from the South to the North,
Led by Kelly the boy from Killan.

Tell me who is the giant with the gold curling hair,
He who strides at the head of your band?
Seven feet is his height with some inches to spare,
And he looks like a king in command.

Ah, me lads, that's the pride of the bold Shelmaliers,
Of the greatest of heroes of man.
Fling your beavers aloft, and give three ringing cheers
For John Kelly, the boy from Killan.

Enniscorthy is in flames, and old Wexford is won,
And tomorrow the Barrow we will cross.
On a hill o'er the town, we have planted a gun,
That will batter the gateway to Ross,
And you Forthmen and Bargeymen will march o'er the heath,
With brave Harvey to lead in the van.

But the foremost of all in that grim gap-of-death,
Will be Kelly, the boy from Killan.
Brave John Kelly, our own boy from Killan.

If you were one of those who heard this bouncing anthem, you'll recognize it now. I hope you'll sing along. [As in the next and final verse we lose, I lose that. No need for you to sing it.]

The American trail transformed this Irish march to:

What's the News?

What's the news? State your views,
Oh, my bold clear-eyed man,
You who holds liberty by the hand.
Tell us why we who cry, "Live free or die,"
Though we try, do but buy into the Lie.

Well, lass and lad, we've all been had.
We never had democracy.
We vote in men who never should win.
Red/blue, young/old, from the same mold
All bought and sold, ready to fold when they are told.

Now the people must tell representatives, "Go to Hell."
Re-presenters is all the public need,
To carry views and bring back news,
Non-partisan and unlobbied,
To your own block, the true bedrock of liberty.
Immediate recall and disavowal
Would keep power all honest and local,
That's what we'd need if we'd be freed,
Not go to our graves, all awful liars and slaves.

If short on songs, I thanked with a joke or an Irish blessing. My favorite joke, brought straight from Ireland, raced up the path ahead of me where it morphed into an Appalachian Trail joke. An Englishman, an Irishman and a Scotsman were transformed into a day-hiker, a section-hiker and a thru-hiker. As this disguise was funnier than the punch line, I can't tell you the joke. You needed to be there anyway.

I did my best to "always leave them laughing when [I'd] say good-bye," except I wouldn't say good-bye. I'd say hello instead, or the Irish greeting, "Dia duit" (Gia ditch) or "God to you."

Am I not a rebel now?

CHAPTER 6

Something Big

Okay, I have guided you down a path, from bear and moose, to the weight on your back or your mind. To everything that might have frightened you, my answer has been: fear God only.
Have we missed anything?

Think big this time. Bigger than a moose. Nearly as expansive and omnipresent as the Almighty, Time and Weather, that He wields mightily, might rightly inspire fear. Be not afraid, not if you've packed as directed, and follow the following itinerary.

To hike El Camino from France requires one month minimum. May, month of Mary, may suit most. You need to be climbing the Pyrenees by October 1st at least. The same first should finish the Appalachian pilgrimage. Baxter State Park, Maine's trail end, closes on October 15th, or anytime the head ranger decides. Unpredictable weather (or funding) can prove prohibitive before then. Even if not legally prohibited, you may prefer to wait a few days for a clear day. Give your ascent some leeway. Delay too long, looking for a pleasanter hike, you may miss altogether.

Only a fool would wait this long to start the sobo hike.

Nobo, October 1st allows sufficient leeway, not only for the Katahdin climb, but to continue to Canada if you steer away from the international A.T. and the mountains. New England did surprise me by the sharpness of its fall.

Ireland is open for hiking year round, but the weather can concern in any season. December, January, and February do not commend themselves for strolling, especially in the mountains.

In America, march in March, month of Mars, traditional opener for military campaigns. As a frigid February might have left you with few bugs even in Florida, march double-time.

No more appropriate starting point than Forte San Marcos comes to my mind. From Appalachee Bay on the Gulf of Mexico, Appalachee injuns ruled the route to the mountains. St. Mark puts you on a paved path north. If you move out on March 1st, not a week later like one fool, you'll easily reach the mountain trailhead by April Fool's Day, still the most fitting day for setting off. "Adelante por Dios, San Marcos y Santiago!"

If you've cleared your calendar, six months should see you over Mt. Katahdin, and over the St. Lawrence, happy as Larry. Unless you've been asinine somewhere, you won't even need to do at-the-double, but don't doddle. My best advice: rise with the sun, sit down at sundown, lie down with darkness. You'll need no help following the white blazes all the way—except for your sanity.

With a little intelligent blazing of your own, you can give yourself some wise breaks, if you don't wander far from the trail. I recommend a week in Damascus, Virginia, mid-May for Trail Days. You'll need to hike into that hiking festival to be on schedule for all the hiker activities on the way. That should still allow for one week in New York, staying out of the August heat. Leave yourself a day here or there for when the weather turns worse than usual.

Maintaining that itinerary, you won't find the weather too bad for more than two days at a time. If hiking at all times you ought to, you won't need to hike when you shouldn't. Don't do as I did. Slow to rise, slower to break camp, running to catch up, I could have killed myself. A worse mistake was hitching far from the trail on various familial duties. That meant hitching back, speeding once more past all the mountains I still needed to clamber or crawl over. Brutal.

A very lucky 13 vehicles, everything from plane to pickup, I employed to circuit as many states. In the open bed of a truck ripping up a Tennessee interstate, I prayed police and precipitation would stay away. Way-hey! Not only did God and troopers not rain on my float, I was sent a second pick-up under the overcast sky. Except for a tear of gratitude (and nostalgia) from this old farm boy, I stayed dry. I think the troopers down here leave the punishment to God for riding old-fashioned in a pick-up.

Understand, you will need to walk in the rain often, and in the snow occasionally. You will get wet. Don't expect to stay dry, you'll stay happier. The fanciest rain gear in the world will not protect. If you shed every drop, you'll be soaked in sweat and be more dehydrated. Expensive space-age suits won't keep their promises. Once an inexpensive poncho has failed you, accept your fate. Just keep truckin' to stay warm. If you keep your pack dry, you'll be alright.

When, finding shelter, you stop for the night, if you find dry clothes and edibles in your pack, plus a less-than-sodden sleeping-bag, you will have beaten a bad day. Harroo-hooray!

Walking-pneumonia is the alternative. Or, even in fine weather, sweat-soaked clothes might sicken you. At all times keep ready one dry change of clothes.

Weatherwise, '09 worked out to be a good year, if you walked with me. I recall thinking time and again, "Thank You, God," for His holding the clouds until I could climb off a cliff. '05 or '07 held the record for rainfall. Thru-hikers wore rain-gear 150 of 180 days (we're told). I could complain but wouldn't. I learned my lesson: never bitch about weather; God can make it worse.

When I shifted a heavy, unsifted pack through Florida into Georgia, the thermometer read 80 to 90 an entire week, the second week in March! Not a bud on the trees offered a blessed smidgen of shade. Sweet Jesus mercy, I sweated away 20 pounds, down to 145, while still hoaking a pack more than one-third of my body weight. In Atlanta, the post office and the Ramada Inn helped me to sweat another 20 pounds from my pack. The Clarion House allowed me to stay for free. That's how pitiful I appeared, from walking there for charity. The Christian folk of South Georgia hurried to help me repeatedly en route.

Still, I objected, belly-ached about the heat wave in what was after all still winter. That's when the rain started. Monsoons would swoosh without warning. Never saw the like. Then, climbing to the mountainous border with North Carolina, a month later, the temperature dropped to 10°F, or 22 below freezing! For three days—without coat, sweatshirt, scarf or gloves (all left in Atlanta)—I stomped through snow over my shoes. As the fourth day went over 70°F, snow disappeared along with all my credibility. Anyone arriving, who overheard my griping, might chide me for fear-mongering hyperbole.

The journal entry at the first Carolinian shelter describes my state accurately:

> *Muskrat Creek, 7 April '09*
> *Arrived last night, long after dark, in a blizzard. Never closer to total exhaustion—in the woods on a mountain, after dark in the snow, without shelter or even a coat.*
>
> *To make me more uncomfortable, I passed at twilight a famously twisted tree which spoke to me of shape-shifting pookas (native to Irish and American culture). Siren voices called from deep forest. Then snow began to fall in flat squares, nothing I'd ever seen before. Like bites of unleavened bread, they reminded me of my hunger when I had little vittles and no time to eat. Finally, finding the shelter full, I needed to pitch a tent in the snow when I was about to pitch over and puke up.*

Having managed to eat something, I found my water bottle icing. My light sleeping bag, also freezing, kept my sleeping light. Yet, for the record, I rose early, to emerge singing from my snowy cocoon, for the entertainment of other poor pilgrims:

"Nothing could be finer than to be in Carolina in the morning."

Oh, the cruel irony in every line! Unbearable. The soft shoe shuffle is easy though in powdery snow.

08 April 09
Also listed under "experiences NOT to be repeated:" beating pants against post to break off ice before pulling them on for another day of galumphing through snow.

Reaching Canada by October took on new urgency on a Carolina April "spring morning." The inadequacy of three-sided shelters had been adequately demonstrated to me. The drawback to packing a light, inexpensive sleeping bag was also drawn boldly. However, a tarp (possibly supplied) helps a shelter, and the lightest blanket fixes the latter problem. Continuous exercise renders coats superfluous. I never complained about heat or cold after that. Only once did I curse rain…

On another morning in Carolina I ran along a high ridge, hoping to reach shelter before rain made me regret not stopping to unpack poncho and pack cover. Pride pushed me, as stopping meant admitting my mistake. As sprinkles grew earnest, I cursed myself, along with the fool in the clearing ahead who failed to comprehend my shouted queries. Let's just call his response questionable, and too typical of our deaf society: "Smelter?" "Skelter?" "Shell Station?" Shithead.

Throwing down my pack in disgust in the slight shelter of a

barren tree, I yanked out my pack cover. This action, done a dozen times before, this time popped out a tiny piece of metal. Catching the glint, with the corner of my eye and my left hand (miraculously), I opened my fist to find a medal of my patron saint. Having no notion how this talisman appeared, I was stunned, but not nearly as much as by the bolt of lighting then striking next to me. The flash blinded my left eye as the crash of thunder deafened my left ear. I could still perceive a witness sprinting from the bushes beside me. "Did you see that?" he screamed, streaking past.

Did I see it? I nearly never saw anything else. Beating down the mountain, half blind, pack and poncho half on and half off, I flew past my new pal, but waited at the foot for him, where I had found the best of "trail magic": chocolate and bananas, another miracle. As the A.T.C. regularly keeps hikers on sparsely sparred ridges in thunderstorms, more *not* being killed is also miraculous.

In a blinding flash the real enemy of A.T. hikers appears. "Treachery! Seek it out."

--- † ---

Before attending to the people entrusted with the lives of hikers, I issue a final warning about Time and Weather. Celebrate Labor Day in Massachusetts or miss out on Maine. Celebrate with hard work before the hiking gets harder. "Vermud" will follow, just before New Hampshire where the cruel joke goes, "Congratulations, you've reached half way!" You have no time to lose while the weather of the White Mountains still waits to waylay you. Some say Maine manages to mangle hikers more. Watch out for rising water there; Maine men don't believe in bridges.

I managed two diary entries in New England:

New Hampshire, 19 September 09, The Hardest Day
The day began easy. I woke early, feeling fine, well rested

on a public bench in a sheltered nook. This roost I'd sought successfully after hearing reports of hard freezing atop the Whites. Re-up pressed me down the mountain anyway. Though no store appeared, the A.M.C. Highland Center laid out delicious food aplenty. Breakfast I could have skipped, had it looked less tasty. Down my gullet the platefuls fell, despite my awareness of the ascent to come, up Crawford's Gully. That historic route to Mt. Washington proved undemanding however. The first stage, Mizpah Hut, I reached without retching, and Mt. Jackson my Old Hickory saluted. The next stage demanded more, but my body responded readily by then.

Even while holding on his hat, this mountain goat was able to run most of the way to the next shelter, "Lakes-in-the-clouds." Two thru-hiker pals behind me spurred my climb, as did my behind needing a sit down. Beating my companions/competition, I still lost, as the hut had already closed for the season. Good news I gleaned from descenders though: a restaurant (with restrooms) rests up top.

Cars and a funicular could from the west defeat the tallest mountain in the East, rendering my climbing even more nonsensical. Damned if I gave a damn. Only 1 1/2 miles of jagged rock remained before the banishment of a bogeyman scaring me (towards it!) for 1,000 miles.

With the hut shut, and the afternoon open, no choice other than pressing onward presented itself. The weather, as good as could be expected in late September, confirmed my decision. Almost perfectly sunny below, the atmosphere above was driven in white mist by winds 50 to 70 m.p.h., producing a -5°F wind chill. As tomorrow could always be worse, I needed, this close, to continue. Pushing me harder was the need to climb down afterwards, down to a survivable clime.

What I had considered good luck (an all-you-can-eat

breakfast) and bad luck (a shut shelter) turned out the opposite. The summit's facilities were attained in the nick of time. All needs attended, all queries answered, I stepped out onto the quickest way down—hopefully.

Briefly on the auto-route, I was driven by heavy gusts into the path of oncoming cars, after the road was supposedly closed to traffic. Having located the correct path off of asphalt, I turned onto the wrong path, onto some seriously treacherous trekking. Only with the aid of previous pilgrims, plus my flashlight and the light of grace, I discovered the way, dangerous and difficult as it was. Finally found in the dark, a clearing large enough for lying down let me rest.

Bracing my staff between two trees prevented my sliding into a creek. Without shelter, tent, bear box or fire—cowboying on my lonesome—I did worry some, but not enough to keep me awake after that long day. Next morning, waking dry and alive, I learned I should have worried more. Nearby, bear-alert posters alarmed, mostly with the threat of "Smokey-the-bear." $2,000 fines might maul me for failing to hang food 10 feet up. The bear threat was not exaggerated this time either. Ol' trail chums, met that morning, reported a bear invading their campground the previous night (the site I'd sought). Yogi helped himself to food bags while the campers prepared supper. Apparently, I was too lost for bears to find me, but when daylight did, it showed the way to town, to hazard-free food and beds.

Once safe and sound, I could recall the long columns of names listed above on the mountain. On a Roll of Error (not of honor) authorities shame the hundreds who've lost their lives in the Whites. Plenty of people, probably better prepared than I, have perished up there among the dead presidents.

Just two days later, the second hardest day was rendered easier solely by more clement weather beyond the dark shadow of Mt. Washington.

*Acknowledged the **hardest mile** on the A.T., Mahoosuc Notch cuts into Maine. The intent, behind pushing the A.T. through there, is clearly to cut the numbers reaching Katahdin. The Gates of Hades comes to mind when faced with this evil jumble of boulders compressed inside a deep gorge. If bolder than the boulders, hikers must clamber over and under, in defiance of good sense or gory fate. A level of hell is confirmed by an unnatural breeze blowing by, the warm and wet breath of the beast.*

If you know Devils' Den at Gettysburg, multiply it by 1000. Imagine while you're at it, 100,000 dens ideal for any wild beast. Know, when the danger is real, a bad notion will snake into your brain. You'll delight in the demise of every bear, wolf, catamount, polecat, rat or reptile shot, trapped, stabbed or poisoned out of those parts. You'll have hiked way past p.c. by then.

CHAPTER 7

The Enemy Within

The A.T. finishes in Maine with the 100 Mile Wilderness before the trail's most serious climb, Mt. Katahdin. Possibly by design, Maine manages to make hikers do long days. On the day that I met a sobo doing a 20-hour day, I pulled off 22 hours. 18- and 20-hour days followed. Discomfort delivers this comforting thought: the trail behind you is only brutal to prepare you for New England. You won't make it to Maine though, if the A.T.C. breaks your body beforehand.

My favorite analogy for the Appalachian Torture Conference goes as follows.

Imagine a general ordered, before the railroad era, to march a regiment from Georgia to Maine. This officer, proud of the stamina drilled into his troops on an obstacle course of his design, decides not to send his men by any rational route. Instead he orders them to the closest base with another obstacle course. Never mind that the base isn't north of his own. The next one isn't either, but the route to there passes through notoriously terrible terrain. As a result of the general's orders, only 10 percent of the regiment reaches Maine within the year, and none fit to fight. Even the army would court-martial such a commander. He should be shot. The A.T.C. would hail him as a hero.

Having afforded some insight into the nature of this nature trail, I may have revealed more of the character of the characters behind it. Generally characterized as "psychopathic-sadists" by thru-hikers, the A.T. Conferees undoubtedly consider that judgment harsh. I agree. "Unthinking and unfeeling" would probably suffice, if "possibly corrupt" might be kept on standby. Lumps of federal, state and local funding, besides charitable grants, underpin the work of volunteer groups "maintaining" trails. Money is distributed between districts according to trail mileage in each. Dealing out dollars grants power; power corrupts.

Money aside, along with the mindless ups-and-downs (m.u.d.s) and zany zig-zags it creates, the A.T. never constituted a proper thru-trail, though sold as such from the outset. A hodge-podge of dilettante hiking-club training courses was wired together to discourage thru-hiking, to limit accessibility to the countryside.

Keep in mind, when this insane course was initiated, elitism, chauvinism and eugenics rose rampant in America, Europe and Asia. One A.T. booster declared to me, "If we made it easier, everybody could do it." Yeah, and that's bad how? Have we not got enough fat Americans yet? A half-dead old mick with a full pack just ran half your crackpot course anyway. The A.T.C. might as well provide a fit path for any fit person.

The inanity of the current monstrosity does appeal to military trainers. Besides troops trained on it officially, Boy Scout troops are suspiciously taught to hike without staffs. For proper military drill, youngsters should be forced to march up and down the same mountain ad nauseam. The Pentagon requires no rational national trail; no such trail should require the Pentagon.

Don't take me wrong. If you're a day hiker who likes to end where you start, who longs to view every vista in your vicinity, the A.T. might be ideal for you. Some sections of the trail surprised me, surpassed my expectations. As part of a national trail, these natural paradigms do not receive the attention deserved. I would gladly march many miles out of my way to take in any outstanding natural feature or historical fixture, if a course can reasonably be charted onward from there.

No thru-hiker needs to pursue every pathetic path in any locality. He should not be required to peek over every peak, however fog bound or treed in. Every fickle spring or trickle falling need not be located. Yet, once at least, we passed without warning within yards of the best vista in that state. A.T.C. prigs elected to display their attitude problem instead. Thru-hikers deserve a well-planned thru-trail. We have places to be, real mountain to see—up in Maine. Show us your best; then let us rest, and let us go.

We have challenged ourselves to tramp thousands of miles. Any hiking club en route should help us, not jerk us around. A difficult path is easily found: just don't look where you're going. A federally funded national hiking organization should be expected to mark a good path, or none. Statistics on the current version declare 600 superfluous miles in the GA-ME, disheartening hundreds of healthy hikers annually, and dissuading countless more from starting. 400 more miles go unaccountably uncounted, wasted in off-trail rambling to distant shelters, water and re-supply. This thousand mindless miles drags down even seasoned outdoor enthusiasts. Only few possess time and money for such benighted activity. Look to the idle rich or the too-poor-to-care. The fault for the body-bruising, mind-numbing battle lies in the great lie underlying this legendary trail, a falsehood perpetuated by its pretentious Conference. The time has come for a thru-hiker to drive home some home truths to the conferees, and, *more importantly*, to potential thru-hikers:

1) No great unbroken swathe of unspoilt natural beauty sweeps from Georgia to Maine. Much A.T. territory has been heavily harvested, repeatedly and recently. National Forests should belong under the D.O.E., not the D.O.A. (Dept. of Agriculture or Dead On Arrival). However, worse than wholesale exploitation is unchecked timber imports, which bring blights

more destructive of forests than are the lumber companies. Go now, to see our real national treasure, while you still can.

2) No prehistoric trail winds through primordial forest. The present pretense only started in 1923. No one who hiked it then (or in the '40s, '60s, '80s) would recognize it now. The A.T.C. alters its creation every year for environmental, fiscal, political or bureaucratic reasons. No aborigine would tread on today's foolish white-man's way. Any pioneer pathfinder blazing this badly would be tarred and feathered if his unfortunate followers ever caught up. A can of white paint does not a trail make. More paint is needed though. Two blazes should always be visible.

3) The Trail might be diverted to delude thru-hikers about clear cutting, or worse, to avoid a town the A.T.C. would pretend does not exist in their "wilderness." Weary, dirty and hungry, the journeyer is led down a green tunnel by white blazes, far from his natural destination. Ten miles later he might cross a highway and a dilemma. Does he hike or hitch-hike to where he should be already, or press on? Can't we cut that crap? Sometimes the trail cuts right through towns, uses tarmac roads; at other times, snobby s.o.b.s disdain to employ perfectly fine old logging roads. The weary hiker must slog through the mud rather than muddy a piker's subsidized ideal.

4) Thru-hikers should be the foremost consideration of the country's foremost hiking association. Thru-hikers do not enjoy being led by the nose over obstacles, silly and dangerous, for some sadist's distant amusement.

5) Your job is to make the trail shorter and easier, not longer and harder, every year. Anyone can make it more trying, without trying, at any time. If desiring a more difficult life, I need only run the route barefoot and backwards, double packed. All thru-hikers must enjoy a challenge: a mountain per day keeps the doctor (and devil) away. Ten mountains per day, or one mountain for days, make a trail body-damaging and soul-destroying, a sin of some sort.

6) So, please lose the attitude. If your local club's section stinks, because you're too twisted or too lazy to lay out and maintain it properly, don't brag about it. Don't title it "The Rollercoaster," "The Jungle," or "The Ankle-buster." Don't post signs: "*Enjoy—if you survive!*" Your evil choices are not even as wicked as you pretend. What's your object? Are you trying to scare Americans away from healthy exercise? Why do you repeatedly ignore good alternative routes, available already, preferring to inflict suffering?

7) If you claim to have a trail, don't show me a trial (sic), full of slippery boulders, jagged rock and flowing water. Almost worse is the opposite. On the A.T. if you walk any considerable distance on a perfect path, straight in the desired direction, your guts start to twist, knowing your legs will shortly head the other way a mile. In order to climb an incline by increment, you'll be ordered to traipse four miles to progress 20 yards. Certainly that ratio helps to control erosion, but so would other constructions less destructive of a mountain or the human spirit. Do not denature one trail section, for aging baby boomers, while monstrous climbs remain lurking ahead.

8) Put up a fit path for any fit person, or shut up and step aside. Just one sensible path, okay? Firm footing headed the right way, without too much concrete or cars, ain't too much to ask. Give us practical and principled. Oh, also, if you can't stand the climb, get off the mountain.
9) If you Conferees actually do experience an attitude change, the four easiest fixes to your very imperfect path are listed in the epilogue.
10) An alternative trail is in the works. Anyone interested in playing a part may contact me. I want a trail for people who like hiking, and who want to like hiking after hiking that trail.

CHAPTER 8

Epilogue

I began in Florida with destiny: my first day's destination (the nearest motel) fate named "El Camino" (in Leon County even). Katahdin was reached on my birthday, and climbed the next day, exactly seven months from the Florida coast. From near 3,000 miles away, that's quite an aim. My final destination, Canada, I attained during my charity's annual festival despite all obstacles in between. Only heavenly help let me reach the border. May heaven heap blessings on each sweet angel. Rough lumberjacks and hunters, one busy businesswoman, might be surprised to be described so. I know each of them would like to know I reached my goal, and survived to praise and thank them. Canadian authorities cut short my foreign sojourn, but only due to divine intervention.

In a gnarly state, I crossed the border into Canada, only to be bounced back, 100 miles away, for no reason. After every effort to cross legally, I discovered legal was not enough for Canadian officialdom. Proper documents displaying a pristine record would not suffice if I was not ordinary. Well, I never claimed to be that. Apparently, an American without a car, walking where usually only lumber trucks trundle, proved too much for bored bureaucrats to let pass (after I gave prior notice).

Though victimized before by vicious officiousness in Canada, I did not curse those who bedeviled me. I thanked God for this deliverance. Someday I will return by a more regular route to Canada and sacred pilgrimage. For now, I had only to finish in a day one fifty-mile flourish to connect all my footsteps, to be off the hook and able to start hitching south, ahead of an early blizzard. When heaven blanketed most of the Northeast, everybody groaned and griped, all but one. I was laughing because I was not walking.

=== + ===

Oddly, mid-way between Florida and Canada, the biggest obstacle—Rocksylvania—I had circumvented entirely. Then, having reached the finish, I returned in November to redo the middle, to prove I was not afraid of the notorious "Ankle-buster Trail," when ankle-biting bugs bit less.

What I should admit is that I should have been more leery. The average rambler ought to be petrified. Pennsylvania does *not* deserve its title, "Hardest State," or even "Hardest Section." Pennsylvania provides many pleasant sections, even after Duncannon. "80 unbroken miles of broken rock" breaking into New Jersey is another broken promise—thank God. However, sections 1 to 5 (New Jersey into Pennsylvania) from Route 191 to 501 (less than one A.T.C. map) do constitute the worst series of sections.

Previously preferring rocks to mud, my feet were beat to hell by a biblical plague of stone. Proper hiking boots would have paid off in this purgatory. The problem springs from the A.T.C. selecting an east-west ridge, formed by the folding of ancient sediment beds. The resulting broken shards of shale topping the ridge provides the poorest surface for long-range hiking on the A.T. Jagged and bruising, unstable and slippery, diabolically foot tripping and body catching, in a word, "ideal" is how the A.T.C. would describe the Ankle-buster. To extenuate the torture, they wind the trail through the rock fields to catch every outcropping, and to miss any logging road offering relief.

If even in this region the rock is not totally unrelenting, its reign does reach beyond in either direction. Yet, without proper boots I walked the whole way in the worst season, when treacherous rocks are covered by slippery leaves, and often by darkness and rain. Even the infamous "knife-edge," I fought with my stick in the black night, and won.

November nights caught me in the Rocky Horror Show because July had set me tramping a wide detour around the heart of Lyme Disease darkness, at the height of tick season, in a bad tick year. Canada, plus a personal goal, beckoned northwards, away from a trail overgrown with tick-harboring greenery. At certain times of year, some districts of countryside should be avoided entirely, as the A.T.C. should warn. Never mind recommending poisons to sprinkle your person and clothes. Their known ineffectiveness, and unknown side effects, limit their usefulness.

More effective than warnings, poisons or preparedness, would be the A.T.C. properly maintaining trails. By early summer, undergrowth overgrows most of the trail. One section in Virginia trail workers ignore entirely in favor of a blue-blazed path everybody takes, or anybody able to buy a good map. If white blazes mark a trail too hard to hike or maintain, they ought to be removed—not left to mislead the unfortunate like me. Shorten the trail to make maintenance easier.

Bound by sacred oath to reach Canada for charity, I admit the Ankle-buster trail gave me pause, and caused me to return when the rocks were worse, but the bugs better. If tick activity lessened, I was still lessoned by the ticks. The demons remained, alive and well, and still biting. One bit of good news about the bad news: by daily detailed checks you can I.D. the fake freckle in your armpit or groin, on the back of your head or legs; with mirrors, lights, and good tweezers, or very personal help, you might remove the tick entirely, and beat the devil.

November '09

Having already seen the end of the trail, I am now gifted with foresight. The worst is yet to come, but certain Canada can be grasped, I fear nothing. Yet, I would opine that the worst mile in the A.T. waits not in Maine, but batters hikers behind me in Pennsylvania's Lehigh Gap. That stretch I would refuse to repeat sobo, or in the rain, in the winter, or in the height of summer. God blessed me with ideal weather for a hike in hell. The weather might easily have been worse all along that hellish ridge.

Thru-hikers can't whine too much, as locals bring toddlers and pets to hike and play among the boulders and sharp stone, the bears and rattlesnakes, the ticks and poison ivy. If my phone had been working, I'd have called the S.P.C.A. or S.P.C.C.

At least the baddest trail provides the best shelters. "The 501 Shelter" ranks first, with four walls, two doors, glazed windows and skylight, even a solar shower. Such luxury on the Ankle-buster is a necessity, as you need to build up or recover your strength. However, typical of the A.T., the most-needed shelters are the hardest to locate. Note this entry from my sparse journal:

11/11/09 Armistice Day

At the 11th hour I set off hiking, seeking the peace only pilgrimage brings. Rage I found instead near Rausch Gap, nearly 12 hours later, six of those in darkness. At 11 p.m. I finally found the shelter, despite the best efforts of the A.T.C. to hide it. Peace can be hard to find, even in pilgrimage, if looking on the Appalachian Trail.

12/11/09

El Peregrino de Santiago has arrived after another engaging game of hunt-for-the-hut. When cold and tired, staggering and stumbling in darkness, that may not be the best time for playing games. The A.T.C., sitting at planning boards, disagrees. Aren't they just a barrel of monkeys? Whee! Same game two nights in a row. They never tire of it.

I lost that game more than once, as most thru-hikers have. Shelters usually squat directly on the trail or nearby on well-marked paths, but are occasionally an ill-blazed mile away. Guidebooks offer similarly uneven help in finding dark wooden structures in dark woods. If the A.T.C. cared at all about thru-hikers, they would quit playing games and implement the following:

1) By adopting better trails (and more direct ones), or better maintaining current ones, especially by cutting back brush and weeds, you would enable hikers to concentrate less on footing or ticks, and more on blazes and shelters—not to mention the scenery.
2) Regardless, white blazes should bring pilgrims to within 12 meters of every shelter. A few reflectors facing the trail wouldn't hurt.
3) All white blazes within one-eighth of a mile of a shelter should be topped by a horizontal blaze. This new blaze would mark the simplest and greatest improvement in the A.T. since its foundation. Stress levels would lower all along the trail. Ergo, I wager the A.T.C. will *not* produce that blaze.
4) Anxiety levels would also lessen if distances were posted more frequently and accurately on the A.T. (not least because shelters would be easier to find).

A.T. mileage markers deliver stand-up comedy, but the joke is on the hikers. Continuing to make measurements with a hand-wheel seems silly for a start. You may as well measure oceans with a wheel. A loose light chain would undulate with the trail, would weave behind a walker to produce more accuracy than a bounding wheel would, skimming air, cutting water, carried over obstacles. Even while the trail is truly shortened, federal remuneration could be increased by one third if proper measurement was taken. Sponsorship for hikers' charities would likewise increase. Moreover, less discouraged, hikers would go still further.

Whatever the A.T.C. decides to do, I whisper to all potential pilgrims, to all my readers, "Do not be discouraged." We are all of us only pilgrims on this Earth, strangers in a foreign land. Milestones will always be false. I did not know this truth until I began wandering. Turned out from settled life, I looked for the way to go, and found The Way came to me.

Because I traveled Europe and studied the past, Revelations, and the future, was revealed. Because I traveled the world, the end-of-the-world-as-we-know-it became clear to me. If I now preach doomsday, my message is yet hopeful, not despairing. While singing of rebellion all along the Appalachian Trail, I offered the warning (at right) from the Lord to all who had ears to hear:

I am not a prophet. I am a pilgrim, a voice in the wilderness, but my field is history, not the future. The Bible I approached as historic historical fiction. I did not come to God through faith, as prescribed. God came back for me, due to doubt. I questioned all; quite unexpectedly, Christ kindly answered me.

If you study history and current events, you know the end-of-the-world-as-we-know-it is very likely near. Man's carelessly evil deeds now bear catastrophic fruit: politically, economically, socially, environmentally. Due to instability in the Middle East, geo-politics teeters ever on the brink. If you never opened the Bible, you could still view our prospects as apocalyptic. No, I won't shout, "Repent and be saved!" Don't run to religion to escape the reality we've all created. Open a Bible as I did, for distraction. Find Luke 21, where Jesus tells the apostles their world will end in their lifetime. Outside the massively impressive temple in Jerusalem, pinnacle of God's covenant with the Jews, Jesus foretells its total destruction. A wrathful judgment is promised on the chosen people: a great slaughter, and dispersal throughout the nations. All came to pass as scheduled…

A new covenant is promised for the whole world. Initially persecuted, Christians were to prosper, but that world would end in turn, after specific signs. First, Israel would return to Palestine; earthquakes and tsunamis would follow, with dramatic climatic change and social upheaval. Lastly, judgment would come "on a cloud with power and glory!" Maybe mushroom shaped?

Climate has changed before, but never while Jews ruled Jerusalem again. How did that happen, and does the world not deserve judgment? The Jews are there due to: (a) the great evil of the Holocaust; (b) the final throw of European colonialism; (c) prior machinations from the British Empire; (d) American support for that empire during WWI, counter to all for which we stood.

Since Washington's presidency, our ideal had been neutrality between European militarists. Our population had largely migrated here to avoid that militarism. The largest immigrant groups were German and Irish. Woodrow Wilson, a Democrat, had been elected primarily by pledging not to mix in Europe's war. Our armed opposition (three times) to British imperialism created our country. Yet, in 1917 we entered the bloodiest war in history on behalf of the largest empire in history.

Why? (a) "To make the world safe for democracy"(!?); (b) "To free small nations"(Ha!); (c) "To avenge the Lusitania"(a British ship sunk two years before, after much warning, while a British blockade crippled our trade); (d) "To end all war"—by breaking a stalemate, crushing Germany, creating Hitler, WWII, the Holocaust, the state of Israel, and militant Islam. While we were at it, we ended the 1,000-year reich of the Hapsburg Dynasty, the Holy Roman Emperors, who had started the Great War. Their rise and fall following Rome's fall (both predicted in Revelations 13) made way for the short-lived Third Reich, foretold, and the last reich to come.

Our inexplicable involvement in the cataclysmic WWI can be explained. Seldom told, the truth is: high financiers ordered Wilson to war, to make the world safe for capitalism. So much American money had been invested in the British Empire, world-wide depression would certainly follow Britain's defeat. Ironically, through continued fiscal mismanagement, the Great Depression befell us all anyway. Now, the military/capitalist complex has combined again with undemocratic government to bring us to the brink.

Do not despair however. Revelations also promises a new order, another 1,000-year reich, built on Christian principle, peace with justice. Let every Christian, every citizen, begin to do his duty: to establish government of the people, by the people, for the people, i.e. God's Kingdom on Earth. If Christ never rose before, He will have risen then. He who is the Truth will set you free.

CHAPTER 9

Post Script: Notes Not Fitting the Narrative

If the A.T.C. did as suggested, they might help to save small-town U.S.A., otherwise doomed. I don't speak of the "Ye Olde Townes" already discussed, more correctly titled "subdivisions." Real villages remain, hanging by a thread (or noose). Individuals must act to save community.

Tramping her back roads, I learned that America is only held together by Subway and Dollar General outlets, more even than by McDonalds and Walmart. The common bond is poverty. If your village cannot support a Subway and dollar store, the time may have come to provide decent burial. Before you die, at least recognize the danger you and yours are in.

--- + ---

The scariest subject not already mentioned, possibly suppressed by my subconscious, would be the A.T. toilet facilities. Ecologically designed to save the planet, they constitute a health hazard to hikers, worse than the more public loos in towns. Even tick-infested bushes serve better. Though state and national parks generally construct outhouses to a higher standard, shelter privies usually will make your lungs gag and your eyes water.

The unacceptable alternative is the un-privy, a wide-open stage for personal performances. Hope for no calls for encores. I recommend doing the necessary before reaching camp. Please steer well clear of water sources. Officially, you're asked to pack in a shovel, and pack out soiled paper. Let 'em tell that to the bears. I should warn about El Camino, however: the lack of facilities, even bushes, can be quite off-putting. Back on the A.T., you occasionally come across proper porcelain unexpectedly in the big parks. I must caution, at the gleaming white sight, you may choke up and shed a tear.

One huge bogeyman you'll never see but always fear on the long trail: bad luck, especially the backtracking kind. However, if you follow the advice outlined in this book, you'll have little cause to worry. People can and do make their own luck. If you don't push your luck, that lady won't shove you back. Not foolishly pushing yourself into a dizzy state of foolishness is the smartest plan. Consider, in the following diary excerpt from way back in Georgia, the foolishness to which I got up.

All the luck I own, I just used up in fifteen minutes. Fussing about in a restaurant, in order improperly to shave in their restroom, I improperly put away my razor. No big deal I thought, and no, I didn't lose it. I just nearly lost everything else in the unzipped pouch where I should have put the razor. I had tramped a mile before realizing, and removing my pack. Only after I'd found nothing missing did I re-hoist the load, to find something missing. On the ground my sacred talisman lay. Had it fallen from my neck at any other time, I never would have noticed.

Even weirder, just as I left the restaurant, barging with all my gear through a difficult door, my phone annoyingly sounded. Searching my many pockets, I found no phone, as it still charged at an outlet inside. In another 10 seconds, I might have been headed 20 miles away. I've left my phone charging before, and lost a day retrieving it, but miraculously did not lose the phone. Another few minutes on that occasion would have put the phone in a puddle. Somebody is watching over me.

If watched, I feel tested too, but carefully. Pushed, I am never pressed totally past my limits. First, the region was rendered too cold for locals, but okay for a hiking northerner. When the weather turned too hot, the previous cold spell had eliminated the bugs which would have tormented me. Once I had acclimatized, the insects were loosed from hell. Between my pack and aching back, a truce eventually was negotiated, just before new pains in my legs arrived.

Speaking of pains in the legs—not to mention unmentionable body parts—nothing hurts worse than one step in the wrong direction. When taking a million steps, retracing one step is torture.

By the hard irony of Irish luck, St. Patrick's Day I spent in Fort Valley, Georgia. Never again. I walked or ran there (considerably out of my way) looking for a bus station. Contrary to all assurances, and at least four signs, no such station exists in this big college town. True, I could still have caught a bus, if I'd bought one. They're manufactured there, though on short hours now. (What did I say about making your luck?)

More surprising, no bar in town was willing to pretend to be an Irish pub, even for a day. Nary a soul was wearing green to celebrate being 2.5 percent Irish. The colleens in the CVS Pharmacy were darling just the same, and gave me kisses (candy ones) for my sharing my heritage by singing.

Maybe here is where I should thank The Kingston Trio for a hard luck song that comforted me along the trail. Called "The Tijuana Jail," it was reworded by the Appalachian Trail.

Well, I went one day/Down to Florida
To have a little stroll/back up to Canada.
I started out/for charity,
But ended up/with insanity.
Chorus*:*
That's where I am/on the Appalachian Trail.
I've got some friends/I must not fail.
So here I'll stay/Till the sponsors pay.
Just send my mail/To the Appalachian Trail.
[c/o General Delivery; hold for thru-hiker.]

Just one cent per mile/would make me smile,
But a dollar per state/would be just great.
I know 30 bucks/Don't sound like much,
but 15 will do, if you're in a crunch.
Chorus:

--- + ---

I shall finish where I began on the A.T., with these scribbles about the first day:

2 April '09
Despite forgetting my stretching exercises again, I covered a good distance today on a tougher than expected trail. Tomorrow had better be better though, if I'm ever to see Tennessee, never mind Maine. I did stay ahead of all hikers passed yesterday. That's not bad considering I began the A.T. barely able to hobble, and bawling for ice and aspirin.
The swelling in my right knee is down; the twinge in my left ankle remains but constant; and the little toe on my right foot doesn't look as bad as it smells. Being crippled at least prevents my walking my way into nausea. I am

inspired to go on by a phoenix rising in the shelter last night.

This bird is not mythological. A very real thru-hiker, "Phoenix Rising" begins her second attempt at the trail. In the meantime she aided others, as a trail angel in Virginia. Bellissimo, her lucient face might inspire a painter, but as a hiker, I'm more motivated by ugly scars from her recent operations. She probably should not be out here, but I am selfishly glad she is. May angels protect her.

I hope I inspired her with my rousing rendition this morning of "Kelly the Boy from Killan" when marching away. Luck let me share the shelter with Phoenix alone. Finding any shelter was very fortuitous. After reaching Amicolala State Park, any hiker still faces 10 miles, mostly uphill to the start of the A.T., including 600 stair steps. "Where in blue blazes will the blue blazes end?" you wonder. If not at Springer before sunset, you'd better spring faster if you mean to reach the next shelter, Stover Creek, a further three miles up the famous white blazes. I did fear having already overshot the shelter in the dark, when a stray tenter directed me to it.

The previous night at the Amicolala hut, I'd also only shared with one (not so bellissimo): a head-banging jarhead from 'Nam, who had tramped the entire country in shoes scavenged from bargain bins or rubbish bins—a lesson to my pride, the second one in two minutes. Rushing to reach the shelter before another backpacker (who never showed), I tripped headlong, unable to catch myself with my staff. The stick did steer me into a leaf pile. No damage done, except to pride. That's a dangerous commodity, especially on the A.T. "Pride goeth before the fall," my Ma would say, and, "From fun comes pain."

Not an auspicious start.

CHAPTER 10

The Link to All Aboard

The Physical Link to

The Last Train to Nowhere
and
Pilgrim's Progress—Possibly

Another woman, fastened forever in my mind to the Appalachian Trail, called herself "Tuesday," as in "Tuesday's child is full of grace." Perhaps this trail name came from a private joke or a pratfall on a rainy, slippery-trailed Tuesday. Whenever I met her, "Wednesday" or "Friday" seemed more appropriate, "full of woe" or "far to go." She was certainly full of chigger bites, having collapsed on a sandy trail, due to being *not* full of food. She had lurched onto the trail, quite unprepared, only looking for a place to die.

She never made her way to Maine, but she did reach redemption. Tuesday left the trail no longer looking for Death. She found hope in the charity granted to her by many, due to their faith, in God and in her. I hope I helped. Perhaps the physical trial of the trail reinvigorated her soul.

Two guys I met again at the end of the trail in Maine. One was the tenter from the first night, noted above. Since he saved me back there, I was pleased to find him in the final hostel, to learn that he too had made it. Phoenix did not. The damn ticks got her, as they would have nabbed me. I know she made impressive progress, and

I know she went with me in spirit to Katahdin's summit. I don't believe she ever made it to Maine physically. Yet, there I found in an A.T. lean-to a book entitled *Phoenix Rising,* an action thriller, whose protagonist is a fine, strong-willed woman. I've no notion where the book originated, but I know it traveled to the mountain top with me, though all excess weight I'd long abandoned. I know the book will go to her if I ever find her.

I think I may. For, the other guy unexpectedly faced in Maine I'd met on the train last year. He recognized me immediately, as we had held much in common philosophically. He had launched himself on a different kind of journey, far away politically from friends and family. Feeling cut off, he seemed anxious to share thoughts with me. As I discovered him hiking sobo, he must have been on another quest, searching for the real America.

I began my peregrinations merely looking for a burial place in Ireland (refer to *A Pilgrim's Progress—Possibly*). Then, God Himself came looking for me, and directed death away—for a time. Looks like I do still have things to do.

American and Australian aborigines famously engaged in solitary walkabouts to holy places, as rites of passage or repentance, seeking gnostic enlightenment (often cheating with hallucinogens). Inducing delirium via exhaustion, dehydration, fasting or other deprevation is not required either to experience visions or visitations. You must just give yourself time and opportunity to observe and reflect, while not stagnating. By depriving your body, you can learn truths about yourself. Yet, more importantly, by denying your mind the usual junk fed it, you can learn Truth about your soul, your non-self.

All the world's major religions have employed pilgrimage heavily as a spiritual tool, none more so than Christianity. Only since the Reformation has this practice declined. All truth was to be found in the Bible, as nothing else could be trusted. Even

Catholics grew more cautious, more sedentary in their practices. Religious wars, national borders and international plagues discouraged the long pilgrimages of old. Modern rationalism and materialism nearly completed their decline.

As the world becomes smaller, but more open and aware, pilgrimage begins to grow again. I may point out that people in The Bible (eg. Jesus) pilgrimaged in search of Truth, and to disperse it.

Before Christianity, Celts in Europe, more than others, used pilgrimage more communally. Sacred pagan places monks transferred to the new religion, for pilgrimage to continue to this day. This would not be the case if the distances traveled did not exceed the miles trod, way more than the miles told on A.T. mile markers.

All Aboard! The Last Train to Nowhere

CHAPTER 1

America

30 June 08

My money is now spent on a trans-Mongolian/trans-Siberian rail ticket: Hong Kong to St. Petersburg in fact. This month-long journey (specifically October) is a 54th birthday present to myself. From St. Petersburg, I need only train to Warsaw in Poland to have completed the last of five final vows: to circuit the Earth on earth (refer to *A Pilgrim's Progress—Possibly*).

As buying this ticket celebrates still being alive, I hope to be so four months from now. Six months ago, still limping from a mad pilgrimage around Ireland and across Spain, I did something really crazy. Two things actually.

First, I struck myself oddly in the upper abdomen. No, I was not fighting, sporting or grandstanding. What damage I've done is done by my own hand inadvertently, for no reason. Embarrassingly. Symbolically.

What damage is done I've no way to ascertain. The blow produced no pain, only an odd sensation, growing to a bloating and tightening in my chest. Did I bruise or bust something essential? Am I bleeding internally?

No one not a millionaire can afford to seek medical care in America for odd sensations. One relative recently attended a clinic for five minutes of attention from a medical tech. Prior to a family gathering, he sought assurance that an odd sensation did not mean his bringing strep to the party. After a long wait for his five minutes and one swab, the patient received no advice, no care, no cure surely, not even a guarantee that strep would not be carried to infants and elders. This care, or his caring, cost him $500, or $100 per minute.

More recently, a friend fainted at home, due to her self-medication for a viral infection. An ambulance was summoned, and a scan required. Released next morning, still infirm and uninformed, she was certain an $8,000 bill had been added to her burdens (reason to feel faint).

Oh, my other bit of foolishness? If my legs heal, I've resolved to walk from Florida to Canada, up the Appalachian Trail in one season. I have not decided yet if that should be before or after crisscrossing the country hitch-hiking. I'm doing that by train already. I'm obliged besides to repeat the medieval pilgrimage to Spain's Santiago de Compostela—but doubled—while aiding fellow pilgrims.

If you've read *A Pilgrim's Progress—Possibly: Hiking to Hell and Back,* you know I follow a vow wherever it leads, whatever it costs.

--- + ---

01 July 08

If you have read the above book, you will also know I've embarked upon another journey, quite against my will. I began a convinced non-believer, not an atheist, but a determined agnostic, while remaining a cultural Catholic. The final page, however, declared from a church (St. James!) in upstate New York:

"As if 1,000 km is not enough, my mind has journeyed further than my feet. Prior to this pilgrimage, I had long since ceased to attend weekly Mass. I vow now to return here next Sunday, and the next, or to a church somewhere.

"You may see me at the back, not going to communion. I am too good a Catholic not to know I am not a good enough Catholic.

I'm still not a believer. I just think the God I once knew is true. If so, I owe Him this recognition or respect. No reward is expected. Faith is required for that; I will live and die a skeptic.

"This far I can go. If empirical knowledge is not enough, then pride remains my Great Sin. But, Christ did have mercy on a doubting Thomas once. I claim no brilliant epiphany on my pilgrimage. I'm not an epiphany sort of guy. If I saddle up, I am riding into Damascus, or the horse had better be dead (for his sake). However, the whole experience was too much, the odd coincidences too many, the unexpected aid too timely, the strict instruction too obvious.

"I dare anyone. Engage yourself in any great physical endeavor, on your own, far from the common distractions of ordinary life; at the end, see if you still think you are alone."

--- + ---

I swore once that no deathbed conversion would catch me in a moment of weakness. I failed to consider the effect the deathbeds of others would have upon me.

My doubts about skepticism began with the death of my dad. Afterwards, a nervous tick in me was noticed at specific times. This possible disapproval, unsought and inconvenient, was brushed aside, but not before being noted. When my Uncle Tom died this year, I was near alone with him at the end. Out of my mouth was drawn the response to the prayer for the dead: "Eternal rest grant unto him, O Lord, *and let perpetual light shine upon him.*"

Sometimes, in other unguarded moments, a plea to God has entered my head. I have always been able to check it, or laugh it off. This prayer I could not take back. My uncle, ever a taskmaster, had surely when alive been doubtful only about me. Yet, I did know what I owed to him now, what he expected of me. That I gave, and did not take back.

Odd events followed. Having kept a long vigil, I felt the need to return to the land of the living, of the ordinary. Arriving home, my first thought was to turn on the TV. John Wayne appeared, reason sufficient to change channels. However, this young Wayne acted in a film surprisingly not seen before. "The Shepherd of the Hills" ran already well into its reels, another reason to switch, yet the remote I did stay, long enough to hear a hillbilly heroine opine: "The first to see a dead man's face is the next to go."

My uncle did not keep me in suspense for long though. As his body was buried, he took his own son, of the same name, who—though far away—had long suffered with him. This cousin was one of several to die of cancer recently, all near my relatively young age.

Most recently, a sister was scythed by the dread same. In her final days, I bore witness to her. When she passed, my first reaction bypassed the traditional Catholic response. Praying not for the repose of her soul, I jumped straight to seeking intercession. No, not because I am selfish, but because I knew my sister is not, I sought her aid. I could sense her waiting, wanting to be her old self, busy and helpful, now that all pain and suffering had been shed. I can feel her helping me now. She is entwined in the life force encircling us all.

I said as much at the eulogy delivered at her parish church, St. Thomas's (Doubting Thomas).

I never expected any of the above, from far-off field or close at home. If not noting it all in a journal, maybe I would not have noticed it properly. When I rejected God, I expected to be rejected if mistaken. Prepared to face the consequences, reveling in free*doom* and responsibility, I never expected God to come looking for me.

=== † ===

With all these interruptions, I failed to finish typing the aforementioned book until two weeks ago. Despite Herculean effort, I failed to finish by the Thursday deadline I'd set. Then, in the final rush, I missed the bus needed to bring the manuscript for copying and binding. As a result, I started to hitch-hike on Friday the 13th. As my book had been all about traveling regardless, I was not bothered.

However, the first vehicle to appear also stopped, though driven by a lone woman. As she pulled from the curb, I discovered my seatbelt on the "suicide seat" was faulty. The driver would pay little attention to the road while she smoked and spoke incessantly about the approaching end-of-the-world. That I was delivered to the door of Staples should be regarded as a miraculous personal triumph over the dark forces of fate.

Satan holds tricks other than broken seatbelts though. I sometimes seem to tread the rim of some deep depression. As my personality is patently manic, my taking the pledge when young was probably the wisest or luckiest decision I ever made. Most credit belongs to my parents. I do still fear falling though. Whenever I have felt myself slipping, I have ever found the energy to take action, to save my soul—at least for now.

---

04 July 08

Yes, yet another journey I entered upon during the course of the previous tome, also unwillingly. That short trip was bound to be a dead end, if I'm being honest with you, and with myself and with Dulcinea. The 4th of July is a good day for declaring independence. It's okay, I don't feel too bad now. My last letter to her I'll share with you.

Dear Dulcinea,
I do confess to taking badly an apparent unwillingness to keep company with me, even for a few hours. When I called

again as promised, my calls went unanswered and unreturned. Still I left a family party early, to be where I might be with you for an hour.

Never minding never meaning much to you, I had already parted with a parting present to prove that point. I only desired to finish nicely, by including you in the progress of a book that had included you. To learn that I meant nothing to you did mock what you meant to me. From wanting you to call, I came to wishing never to speak to you. Even cruel comments would be foolishly futile against your walls of apathy.

Without word from you, I went alone to a sacred place I had meant to share. There, in the midst of Mass, I realized I could not harbor ill feeling towards you—not fairly. As peace sailed into my heart, my cellphone rang, disturbing the peace of others.

Yes, I'd forgotten to turn off my phone. Muffled in my bag, the ring tone was stifled quickly. Even when Mass was over, two tasks remained before my phone could be opened: 1) turning over the manuscript to a certain monk; 2)lighting a candle for you. (That was a $2 candle!)

You're no cheap date, even in absentia. The real religious experience waited for me outside the chapel when I heard your voice upon my phone. Your message even offered innocent explanation. Do I even care if it's true? Not if you cared enough to call and lie.

Here at this mountaintop monastery, blessed by birdsong and sunshine, peace now reigns.

In a glorious, joyful, sorrowful mystery,
Michael

P.S.: Though left stranded up a mountain, I had no difficulty hitching home, by the grace of God. By odder coincidence, I had to write today to another woman to deflect her attentions. I understand.

═══ + ═══

06 July 08; St. James' Church
I came to church today with an openness not felt before, and found the congregation opening itself for an enfant boy who had commandeered the service—not in a bad way.

Totally atypically, High Mass was turned over to celebrating this beatific toddler's inclusion in the family of faith. At regular intervals, the rites of baptism were woven into the fabric of Mass. Odder still, the child (no relative) happened to have my father's full name.

When the entire congregation was asked to join in renewing their baptismal vows, I discovered being able—for the first time in 35 years— to join in wholeheartedly. When the service was over, I sought out the family to offer the child God's blessing in Irish. Then, I caught up with the priest, to ask for the sacrament of reconciliation.

Dia 's Padraig duit,
Michael

═══ + ═══

08 July 08
In the year that Barack Obama is the first black Democratic candidate for president, we should look back, to precisely 80 years ago, one man's lifetime, to 1928, to when Al Smith was the first Irish or Catholic presidential choice for the same party (or any major party). Because of bigotry, Smith's election was never likely; *because* Obama is black, he's expected to win.

My father was old enough to follow the campaign in newspapers then. Later he often recalled a columnist reporting from Nashville: "Most folks in Tennessee have never seen a Catholic, but they have a pretty good idea what one ought to look like." The Dems lost the South, for the first time since the Civil War.

Mother was nine, still in grade school—not in Tennessee—in upstate New York, Smith's own state, when her public school teacher elected to celebrate Smith's defeat by offering this lesson: "Anyone who would cross himself, would double-cross anyone else." Hopelessly ignorant papist supporters of Smith in her class were told they might just as well go home.

At that, Mother collected her younger siblings by the hand, and set off for home, two miles away. Only then was her teacher taught that maybe she had gone too far. One of the big boys was sent to "urge" Mother back to school.

The final irony of this story is that Mom will *not* be voting Obama, not due to any prejudice of hers, but because the Democratic Party and its candidate decided long ago to be anti-Catholic. Once, the R.C. Church had been that party at prayer. For the "liberal" factions who usurped power in "the People's Party," for all relativists, Truth must be relative, except for relativism. From the truth that there's no Truth, no dissent can be allowed, nothing decent even, only descent.

Nearly 90, Mother will be voting Republican, for John McCain, a true descendent of the W.A.S.P.-ish race that hounded her youth. Isn't that very open minded and liberal of her?

Author's note: *On my next trip, after Obama's election, I would pass through Greensboro, N.C., scene of the famous civil-rights sit-in at the Woolworth's lunch counter. The reporting of this dramatic demonstration forms my earliest memories of current events. How amazing that within 50* years an African-American should be sitting in the Oval Office as our president?! Almost as remarkable, Woolworth's no longer exists.

--- + ---

10 July 08 A Summary

I will answer now the questions which I intend to ask of others while en route around the world.

1) *Where are you from?* Ireland. Though I was born and raised in Amerikay, as were my parents before me, I am from Ireland. Even had I not spent most of my life in Ireland, I would still be from there, because my mother raised me in the Old Dark Religion, and the still darker folk memory, and in the shining faith of freedom. Meanwhile, my Da cultivated in me (and in my five brothers and five sisters) the sacredness of soil, and of duty.

Though farm fed, and small-town bred, I am a New York City boy, as only a non-native can be. In N.Y.C., I boarded this train.

2) *Why are you here?* To get where I am going—on the physical and metaphysical planes. First, I'm headed to San Francisco, by an extremely convoluted route, and then around the world—by train. Moreover, I am bound towards completing a sacred vow. In a moment of whimsy, a solemn oath was given to circuit the Earth on earth. As my wife had left me, and my job let me go, I determined (having nowhere to go) to go everywhere, and to write about it, before my health deserts me too. I've left it late.

Included in the oath, and already completed, was a hike entirely around Ireland (before it dies), bit by bit, every inch connected, every foot on foot, before hoofing the last great medieval pilgrimage: from France, across Spain to Santiago de Compostela.

By boarding a train now, I'm actually allowing my legs a rest, before hiking the entire Appalachian Trail (and more) in one season. Possibly pushing a political movement while I go, I may also criss-cross the country hitch-hiking.

On a higher level, my reply remains, "To get where I am going." In words of St. Columbanus: *"Since we are travelers and pilgrims in the world, let us ponder on the end of the road that is our life; for the end of the road is our home."* According to the Catholic catechism, I am here "to know, love and serve God," but I must first know, love and serve myself, as Plato enjoins. If I do so, if I live life consistently, i.e. morally, I will find God, the conscious life-force of whom we are all a part, unless we are apart, doomed and damned.

3) *Where are you bound*—between this train and the train to Glory? I don't know, and that does scare me. I have no prospects, and no retirement or health plan. That makes me typically American. So the question becomes: where is this country bound, and the world with it? My world vision is even bleaker than my personal prospects. Average Americans are not in control of their destinies, not individually or nationally or internationally. Who would even bother to deny that our democracy is an expensive sham (costly materially and morally) shielding the machinations of the wealthy white elite that has secretly steered the world since the Middle Ages?

Call this conspiracy what you will: Templars, Masons, Illuminati, Bilderburgers, Bohemians, Committee of 300, Republicrats. Occasionally, congressional committee or high court covers it. I call "them" the Chauvinistic, Lording-over, Underhanded Bastards. You name them, just don't deny them.

Since the recognized rulers of the West, kings and popes, helped the Templars (and Teutonic Knights) to plunder the East, and then to organize, throughout Christendom, the first international banking system, ordinary citizens have been at the mercy of religious orders organized to wage war and to colonize. As these blood-soaked brotherhoods accumulated wealth and power, they acquired their own religions and agendas. Royalty and papacy, never more powerful, joined forces to suppress dangerous heretics in 1307. Too late.

The Templars' arrogant chauvinism had already lost the Holy Land. Their power, concentrated then in Europe, official suppression only forced underground. Royalty and papacy would be made to pay for betrayal. Since this supposed suppression, the history of the world—religious reformation, social rebellion, national revolutions, international conflicts of empire or ideology—has all amounted to one gigantic fraud, particularly the "rise of democracy."

The only citizens controlling their own lives, the powerful few and the deliberately powerless, we'll call the select and the elect. The morally bankrupt rich run the system from which the religious poor opt out. Ironically, only the Amish can now be seen as truly forward-looking and freedom-loving.

The time has come for all of us to become as radically revolutionary. We have been unwilling to pay the real price of freedom. Buying wholesale the bread-and-circus lifestyle offered by prior empires, we grow weaker by the day while still exploiting others, and sowing a whirlwind of hatred. For the love of God or humanity, are you willing to sacrifice for self-sufficiency and a truly democratic community?

Now we enter desperate times regardless, maybe the end times biblically foretold. What exactly that means I don't even want to know. Demonstrably, the prophesied destruction and resurrection of Israel in Palestine did not portend well for the world. Our outlook grows grimmer by the day. For a cabal of crusaders to bring the whole world back to the Holy Land for destruction is only proper and poetic.

More threatening than nuclear holocaust or electro-magnetic blast, cataclysmic climate change arrives, as also prophesied. Worse still, economic collapse, engineered in the USA, already grips the vulnerable. Our currency lies completely at the mercy of our enemies to the east. Our own power elite already transferred wealth and operations to where currencies are stronger and democracy even weaker. The rise of China makes the American market less important, and its manipulation less worthwhile.

Another prophesy, of a secular sort, academically opined (allegedly in 1787, at our constitution's birth): all great civilizations only last about two centuries, as all fatefully repeat an inevitable progression:
1) from bondage to spiritual belief;
2) from belief to courage;
3) from courage to liberty;
4) from liberty to abundance;
5) from abundance to complacency;
6) from complacency to apathy;
7) from apathy to dependency;
8) from dependency to bondage.

The good news? We never were as free as believed, and we've already arrived at the final stage. We can now begin anew to rebuild a great democracy upon high ideals. That trumps a great hypocrisy, founded on lies and conspiracy, slavery and genocide.

08 August 08

The following presents my clarion call, not to arms but, to peaceful revolution. I will distribute it now to every household in the neighborhood which I choose to be mine should chaos come calling. At minimum, we can select spokespersons, or democracy watchdogs, when tyranny threatens. While the current constitution holds, prudence suggests the people only try to regain control of it. Should public order collapse, we should not make the same mistakes that landed us where we are now. I suggest the system below to keep the reins of government tightly in the people's hands, not vice-versa.

Hard times are coming, but they don't need to be bad, if good people organize. Before the entire nation slides into chaos or dictatorship, shouldn't our declared ideal, *democracy,* be tried once? Before the flare goes up, before so-called political, economic and social order falls, shouldn't we at least return to the old constitution? (Ron Paul's *Revolution*) Of course, if we're really serious about government *of the people, by the people, for the people*—and if the constitution cannot be saved in time to save us—ordinary citizens will need to create a new order from their own localities. While technology remains to help us, shouldn't we organize now?

Every neighborhood should annually elect a spokesperson to learn and re-present his neighbor's views, not misrepresent for personal or party gain. Corrupt career politicos and dirty, lying campaigns are *not* prerequisites of democracy. The only requirement is every neighborhood naming a neighbor who is honest and wise, active and articulate. *If one just man cannot be found, we deserve our fate.*

The job of a street rep is simply communication: convincingly stating the will of his constituents, and reporting back the opinions of others. Whatever cannot be accomplished by open compromise and cooperation should not be done. *Nothing less is liberty.*

Street reps could nominate a village mayor for confirmation by popular vote; mayors could nominate district ambassadors to the federal government (the United Counties of America). Every elected official would be bound by the same democratic principles, or face immediate recall. Each must also know the needs and resources in their area. Less government, but more governance, is needed desperately by society.

We don't need overlapping, uncontrollable, unaccountable, corrupt, costly bureaucracies. Since many Americans died for freedom, why do we submit to party hacks and petty dictators? What can we do? For starters, campaign for constitutional conservatives or libertarians, not neo-conservatives or liberals. Secondly, elect a street rep. Thirdly, get online, or, better still, find or found venues for local views: penny-saver newspapers, community coffee shops or bookstores. Get reading, and get ready to be a *citizen*.

Please ensure every adult in the house reads this manifesto. Seal in a plain envelope one nomination each, of anyone living on your block. Close envelope in front door by 7:00 p.m. Sat. All are welcome to join in collecting. Meet on the steps of the church *before* 7:00 p.m.

- This election is without party or personal gain. None of the above even seeks your vote.
- All were recommended by neighbors as honest, civic-minded citizens.
- If this exercise in community-building grassroots democracy serves no other purpose, all of the above have been honored now by being on this ballot.
- Yet, one must be selected. No campaign need follow though. Judging by their lives, who seems the most active, articulate and truthful to you? *Number your top 3 choices.*
- Each adult may write out a ballot. All will be collected tomorrow after 6:00 p.m.

- If you will be away or busy, seal the ballots in an envelope closed in your front door.
- Anyone wishing to collect and count ballots may meet outside the church before 6:00 p.m.

--- + ---

Mayors could also nominate a District Chairperson to remain in the county seat, in constant touch with mayors, the County Tribune, and with Chairs of other counties (congressional districts), 500 in all. The job of the Tribune and the Chairs is the same as the Street Rep: to re-*present* the decisions of their constituents. The job of those constituents, the citizenry, the people, is to govern. All legislation should originate with ordinary citizens petitioning their street rep, who would approach the town clerk to draft a bill for the mayor to present to the people. If successful in a town, legislation could be presented to the County Chair, where success could commend it to the Federal Congress. Another bureaucratic boondoggle at state level, costly in coin and concern, becomes totally superfluous.

Bills which reach Congress, after coordinating rewrites by county clerks, would be re-submitted by Tribunes to their grassroots. Tribunes must then vote accordingly. If passed above, a law must be accepted below, unless it can be overturned, as unconstitutional, or postponed for two years. The body with the power to do this should be the Senate, formed as follows:

At the close of every term of Congress (two years), the Tribunes of each of the country's ten regions would elect two of their number to remain in Washington with two others elected from the County Chairs. Lastly, any special interest within a region could put a candidate on a regional ballot. From this field, citizens could number their top three choices. #1=3 points, #2=2 points, #3=1 point. The most points wins, presenting the country with 10 more senators, totaling 50. Besides citizens retaining the powers of immediate recall and vote disavowal, term limits would prevent the corruption of elected officials.

Senators may present legislation to the House of Tribunes, but their principal purpose would be to vote down any law anywhere, if they judge it unconstitutional. Alternatively, they may vote merely to postpone, until the next congress also supports the legislation. If all of a Region's senators still oppose the extension of a bill to their Region, it should not hold authority until a plebiscite is held. If the plebiscite fails, the only recourse of the federals would be to re-write and re-submit, or to censure the Region. Instead, they could accept rejection.

The first job of every Congress would be the election of speakers in the House and Senate. Their task, besides presiding over Congress, would be informing the president of the people's will. That executive could be impeached and removed by simple vote in Congress, for failure to execute its duty.

Selected originally by the Senate from their outgoing numbers, the President and his cabinet would face confirmation by the House, subject to their constituencies. The sole qualification: the candidate should be an able and trustworthy executor of the people's will.

At term end, if not impeached, the ex-executive will join the National Council, from whom the new president must pick a V.P. The veep would serve as chief envoy and figurehead.

--- + ---

I'm pleased to announce: the True Democracy Club has been founded, with only one belated phone call from a polite policeman.

--- + ---

14 August 08

Within the week I bused to Boston to conduct a symbolic launch for my mini-manifesto. Boston, home of the Tea Party revolt against taxation without representation (1773), is a particularly appropriate starting point for my revolution. From here I mean to travel by train back and forth across the USA proselytizing democracy. First I need to conduct my own tea party. For that I've brought one copy of the manifesto and one tea bag, fine organic tea. Just off Congress St., I'll throw the tea in the harbor, and the leaflet to the nearest bystander.

--- + ---

Done. My next stop now is New York City where my China visa should be waiting with my passport at the Chinese embassy. Here's hoping. I'll need a visa for Russia too, before embarking on my rail odyssey, as my next stop will be Hong Kong train station. Oddly the wee tea bag just discarded means more to me than all the tea in China. My trip there is anticipated with some trepidation—by me. Every brook and breeze is reportedly caustically polluted. Even normal bacteria and pollen will be completely foreign to me, as will the language, customs and culture (social and political). The entire prospect does not appeal to me, but I can't claim to have traveled the world without seeing China. The Great Wall alone could claim the right to my attention, as the sole man-made construction visible from space, besides the N.Y.C. dump. The latter constitutes more destruction than construction.

--- + ---

15 August 08

Traveling through New York Port Authority, a Mecca for thieves, I have good reason to be concerned. Let's just say my baggage is more precious to me than usual. Even these scribbled notes are as irreplaceable as banknotes. Some of what's carried could raise police suspicion, though not illegal.

Worse still, I need to hang around this neighborhood for hours, until the Chinese embassy opens (also on 42nd Street), before high-tailing back for the 10:00 a.m. bus upstate. The ticket for that had best be bought first, in preparation for a sprint finish.

I confess to forgetting that today is a Holy Day of Obligation, or that an old church hides near Times Square's cross. My timing is perfect for Mass. Parking in an empty pew, I find St. Pat in stained glass above me. Protestant readers may feel uncomfortable around holy days, Catholic saints, and the Whore of Babylon. I only know I feel at home, and at peace here. God surely is at work. Moreover, the Roman Church is not the only one to prostitute itself for worldly wealth and power. The many Protestants practicing religion to improve their standing in society, will burn with the poor papists.

If you would like to learn something about the old religion that formed me, consider this anecdote (or antidote). Don't imagine it typical though, of this century or the previous.

> *Imagine first a small boy, seven years old, maybe eight, anxiously waiting outside church (in 1961?), wanting to go home, while his parents yak interminably at the door. Finally started, they stop again, to shop for groceries. Unusually, the greedy child desires no treats.*
>
> *His stomach he unsettled that morning by the regular rush for Mass. Undoubtedly he wolfed breakfast, or missed it, under pressure from fasting rules for communion. Hell, he always bolts grub. Inevitable after-mass tag games may have added pressure, as did jostling in a crowded car, bumping down a dusty lane. Pulling up to the farm, everything comes up—to land on the station-wagon floor.*
>
> *Almost immediately, the mother remembers Communion*

received. Twenty minutes may have passed, close to the cut off. The volume of vomit suggests not close enough. The question, "Why would anyone accept the sacrament when sick?" hangs around unanswered. The priest is phoned. His instructions: wipe up the mess with a cloth, preferably linen, which must then be burned.

An Irish linen tablecloth, prized wedding gift, a tearful mother sacrifices for dirty sacred duty, before a stern faced matriarch assembles the entire family (father, five brothers, five sisters), after lighting a fire in the dining room fireplace. Kneeling, all are led in a lengthy rosary, beseeching God to spare a small boy's soul from the fires of hell, from flames like those consuming a soiled tablecloth.

The sorry soul is finally returned to church for a special session of confession.

More liberal or fundamental readers may find this tale strange or silly. Do not think I learned no worthwhile lesson however. A child learned of his mother's concern, maybe misguided, for his eternal salvation. Even a rascally boy was impressed by the sincerity of a mother's faith, by her willingness to sacrifice, from love for her Immortal Father and her mortal son.

✠

11:00 p.m.

My prayers were answered today. Not only is my visa obtained (the final obstacle before embarking on circling the world), I returned safely and timely for the bus home, and even found a first cousin directly before me in line. Such encounters typify the small town called New York.

Yes, I did poke her in the back. "Stick 'em up." No, she didn't think it funny either.

30 August 08

I've recently failed again the same endurance test flunked before the previous pilgrimage. A mile-long swim across a lake seems to have fallen foul of my odd adrenalin glands. Well, I didn't drown. Yes, a new vow is now taken.

02 September 08, Tuesday

On the eve of my departure (or destruction) I was unpacked and unwell. Now packed, I'm still not ready to go. I have a building to buy, and a will to write. That involves two separate lawyers, turtles of the professional world. Appointments have been set at least. All remains possible, and that was hard enough.

Worse, my insides are killing me. For two days I've been shitting green, like I'd chowed down nothing but grass for a week. What does it mean? How have I poisoned myself? Is this a stress-induced liver malfunction? If not excess bile, isn't green a sign of severe malnutrition? I have no medic and no medical coverage, no money and no time anyway.

03 September 08, Wednesday

Being Irish, I like green, but I'm drawing the line here. Good news? Seems I've passed the grass and most of the weakness and lethargy that accompanied it. I woke early this morning, before the alarm, to find my adrenalin pumping.

Every task I approached with energy. Though I may be getting old, all jobs were accomplished (if not in orderly fashion) against all odds. I scribble now aboard a bus bouncing into New York. Only now am I recalling small matters unfinished. There's no going back though. *Adelante.*

P.S.: It's started already. Forced by my bowel to use the bus loo, I afterwards found my seat occupied. For the second time in a row, a bus journey has included someone sitting down next to my belongings. Who does that? I can't carry everything into the cubicle. My gear should save my seat when other seats are open. This is just another example of the malfunctioning of society, causing a rise in bile.

---

04 September 08 NYC

To show that I'm still traveling the hard way, carefully rationing cash, I just crossed the Big Bad Apple twice, by subway and city bus, by night and day, while carrying my world (and $1,000) on my back. Though not directly threatened, I reached my sister's Long Island home with relief. It felt like a refuge, due, not only to strong locks or comforting familiarity, but to my sweet sister's presence. This morning, didn't she volunteer to help me on my way, though late herself? No, I did not take advantage, but hoisted my heavy load for the hike to the bus stop.

I can feel a weakness coming on me, but am comforted by a sister's concern. Once on the street, geared up and in gear, I repeated aloud an old refrain to myself, "Steel up, boy, steel up," and sang one verse of "Kelly the Boy from Killan."

What's the news, what's the news, oh, my bold Shelmalier,
With your long barreled gun from the sea?
Say what wind from the south blows its messenger here,
With a hymn for the dawn of the free?

Goodly news, goodly news do I bring, youth of Forth.
Goodly news shall you hear Bargey man.
For the boys march at morn, from the south to the north,
Led by Kelly, the boy from Killan."

Sis's neighbors might think me mad; I should show more consideration for her, if not for them, but the rousing chorus helps me, definitely helps me.

=== + ===

Even from the end of the E-line, I had to stand all the way into Penn Station. The game is now on, and I'm winning so far. Despite the slow, cheap route in, and slight detour to the post office, I'm well ahead of departure time.

I did nearly suffer a heart attack. Checking the valuables pouch, I found $250 could not be found. Not panicking, I removed the pouch to look properly, and discovered a security feature. If inserted in the inside pocket, money slides down far enough to disappear if other pockets are fully expanded. Great, I'll put a packet of tissues on top now, and breathe again.

=== + ===

Another stroke of good fortune! I have been kicking myself for failing to include New Orleans on this rail ride. This morning, I'm told that service has been cancelled due to hurricanes. Wouldn't that have been a fine start?

=== + ===

11:00 a.m.

Well, I am aboard, past the first stop, underway to Elkhart, Indiana, via Washington D.C., before continuing to Washington State. Now safe, I may do something risky. What is the point of criss-crossing America, getting to know the country better, if I don't introduce myself? So, in a few minutes I intend to stand up and do the following: (1)Sing the above Irish rebel verse; (2) Assure all I'm not a crazy busker escaped from the subway or other asylum; (3) State I'm just an Irish boy crossing by train this continent, and the next one, and the next; (4) Announce *not* looking for dollars, just for other Paddies or pilgrims; (5) Say I also seek anyone with a penchant for politics and philosophy; (6) Insist all violence be reserved for the chessboard, where prizes await; (7) Declare even greater interest in players in the publishing game; (8) Lastly, question all fellow passengers in this election year: "If you were elected president, or dictator, what's the first thing you'd do or undo?"

11:00 p.m.

Okay, I never did do the above, because that train was basically a glorified commuter service, on which everyone not asleep was on his cell phone. By the time I readied, the time remaining seemed too short to try. On the next train, from Washington, I was able to find the very crowd sought, without making a spectacle of myself. But don't think I won't, if I have to.

Spectacle is provided here by the Shenandoah Valley near the mountainous and momentous Harper's Ferry. Oohs and aahs crowd the observation car, even from those who cannot see the history of this quaint old town. Even quainter, though, are the many Amish and Mennonite passengers aboard. May God keep them strong for the bad days ahead. May He keep the railroad strong enough to serve His servants until the day of reckoning.

Elkhart, Indiana, 05 September 08

Off the train for a day, 7 a.m. 'til 7 a.m. tomorrow. My first discovery—cruelly—is the loss of a sacred talisman. Not a good sign. Too much grappling with heavy gear broke a medal loose. Kinder was the rediscovery of family far from home. The latter will probably cause me more harm though, as I've eaten too much of food I probably shouldn't touch. It wasn't home cooking, but it was good cooking: IHOP and Golden Corral (the best of buffets, i.e., inexpensive all-you-can-eat eateries). All during eating my money's worth, I knew a bigger price would be paid later.

While still alive, I am most pleased to have visited during this grand tour the grave of my sister, the first to pass, and far from home.

=== + ===

Illinois, 06 September 08

Yes, I did make the train which was just nicely late, and kindly provided a laugh right away. The conductor had me scrambling to find the seat most convenient to him. I might have complained but I noticed he left notes above several seats: "S O B." Whether that stood for whiner or son-of-a-bitch, I didn't know. Turns out, it only abbreviated the next stop: South Bend. I didn't whine anyway.

=== + ===

Chicago 9:00 a.m.

A word of warning about Union Station: luggage lockers are $4.00/hour for the small ones! Have baggage ready for check-in, as that's free. The weight on my back now weighs on my mind. I only forwarded one very heavy bag as far as Minneapolis, as the train stops there for 20 minutes, long enough to reclaim luggage—if it gets there, and I get there. For now, I'm off to see the Windy City, and feeling light and free.

Second surprise: the city provides free regular transport around the city center. I was enabled to roll from Soldier Field to the Navy Pier (and back to Union Station). This city impresses, on this warm summer day at least—bold, beautiful and bustling. Thronging the streets are female professionals (not professional females)—bold, beautiful, without too much bustle. I also liked the well-built Public Library, the Civic Opera, and the Carbide and Carbon Building.

Soldier Field, part of a war memorial complex, fits in nicely with museums and planetariums. All very clean and litter free, the city appears safe and prosperous. No sign of the grim times forecast, except a clever t-shirt message: "God is nowhere." That turned my head for a second look, which revealed: "God is now here," fitting my apocalyptic views.

=== + ===

Major General John Logan's equestrian statue is stirringly martial in the shorefront park stretching north from the stadium along Lake Michigan. This location for civic parades belongs today to Mexicans, led by two very lively equestrians. In tandem the horses march, high-stepping to dramatic drum and bugle music. Just two buglers carry different horns in each hand.

Segway scooters provide an alternative parade along Chicago's waterfront. Looks like the best way to go. Opposite the Logan monument is the Chicago Hilton, imposing and stirring in its own right. This might be the flagship of the Hilton chain. A quick admiring snoop cost me the next bus downtown however. That may just cost me more than I can afford.

Chicago boasts more impressive buildings than New York even, and must be recognized as the father of skyscrapers. The gothic Tribune Building is my favorite, decorated as it is with stones from other famous structures, for example, David's Tower in Jerusalem, the Parthenon, the Taj Mahal, Notre Dame, Westminster, Cologne Cathedral, and most appropriately, China's Great Wall. I, however, preferred a blackened rock from the old General Post Office in Dublin, circa 1916 and the Easter Rebellion.

Patrick Henry's church was also represented, where he let loose the famous, "Give me liberty, or give me death." That quote is inscribed in the lobby, along with 100 others about the freedom of the press. Most of it grandly presents a bunch of hooey. The People should not be dependent on the venal whims of press barons for protection against the abuses of government. Rather, citizens should be able to depend on their own government to defend them against the excesses of a press motivated solely by profit and power.

Oh, shit. Could be trouble. I took one trolley too far. My watch must have switched to the wrong mode. You find me stalled in rush-hour traffic and deep shit. I may not return to the train station in time, and there's nothing I can do about it.

I reached the station just in time, just in time to be told I needed to come early for boarding. None of that last-minute running along the platform is allowed anymore. As most trains originate in this rail hub, the schedule means what it says here. That means I'm swimming in manure for now. Aside from my entire itinerary being flushed, my big bag sits aboard the train hurtling towards St. Paul. I've been informed at four different counters (boarding desk, info desk, ticket counter, and customer service office) that I have no recourse whatever, no means to catch up with my baggage or itinerary. Only one train runs per day, and no room can be found on tomorrow's service, or the next day's. My tickets just turned into turds in my hand. Amtrak allows no room for error, except theirs. "Neither don't take no cigar smokers, this train." I sure ain't bound for glory. The best surprise of the day gave birth to the worst shock. Free trolleys downtown made me miss my expensive train out of town. No hope has been offered me.

Not one to take no for an answer, I approached another ticket agent with another query, which I couched in the hard-luck story of a poor lost traveler from overseas. A seat was found for that pitiful fellow on the next day's run. Some Amtrak employees seem to have seats at their discretionary disposal, for emergencies. Bless all who saved me from train-travel limbo. I'll be "back on track" with my itinerary by tomorrow night. I must credit myself for never saying die, and for originally scheduling an extra, expendable stop. Glacier National Park in Montana will need to wait until another time. I hope the grizzly bears aren't too disappointed and hungry. Maybe God is looking out for me, as I was unable to bring the big can of bear mace given to me. Moreover, I get to blow around more of the Windy City.

The highlight of my Chicago sojourn might just be the Navy pier, which could not have been enjoyed had I made the train. If on the pier you pirouette, the entire skyline presents itself, while on the lake a five-masted schooner may glide by. All around you, fun activities and food are offered. The place is awash in sailors in freshly starched whites. Oddly, the Navy holds a huge base on this freshwater lake. The sailors sure seem to enjoy the city and the lake. Nothing's surprising there.

---

07 September 08

I'm glad I missed my train now. Not only did I get to see much more of Chicago yesterday, today I found my new favorite building here: St. Pat's Church. Built by famine Irish, it was one of the few buildings to survive the great fire of 1871.

I don't feel too bad about missing Glacier National Park. Much has been heard of its beauty, but also of its beasts. Nothing was heard about transport within the park, nothing to ensure my catching the next train out. Instead of being stuck camping with bears, I was able to see more of my kind kindred folks. A little heartache at Union Station may have just saved me a trainload of real pain. The absence of my bear-mace, I accept as a sign from God.

Minneapolis

Well, here's a mark for where our country has fallen. Just after 10:00 p.m., the train pulled into town to hang around for an hour. Off I leapt in search of food costing less than four times normal prices. Managing to find a McDonald's nearby, I also discovered its doors locked, but did not despair as the drive-thru clearly operated. I would need to swallow, however, that no one can obtain food unless he has a car. I understand the policy, I only point it out as a measure of the feverish temperature our sick society has reached.

Never mind, somewhere else was properly open, and served fast food fast enough to return me to the train on time. More good news, my big bag of belongings did indeed wait for me in Minneapolis, as promised. What a relief!

08 September 08

I'm disappointed, surprisingly, in the scenery of this brown season. Maybe I am spoiled by the varied greenery and scenery of Ireland, but even in Eastern America the topography and vegetation varies much more than here, and will shortly burst into color. Even when mountains are finally attained, my eyes are treated to nothing but conifer spars. You need to escape the Cascades to spy real scenery again.

Of some help in spicing up the plain plains, volunteer guides from the National Park Service provide commentary over the PA system. Their patter proved interesting at the time, if not memorable. They at least kept us on the look out for Indians, buffalo and mountain goats. Nothing more than a tepee or two ever entered our view, except for two llamas.

Chad, a clever acquaintance collected on board, with other

card-playing revolutionaries, manages to keep the traveling interesting. Some fellow travelers even voiced interest in buying my travel book!

≡≡≡ + ≡≡≡

Seattle

The Space Needle requires $16 to ride its elevator, not very uplifting, and I wasn't that interested. However, down on the ground, the city does embrace and uplift the visitor, just as its shoreline embraces the uplifting sea. Bluffs above the bay remind unexpectedly of vistas Mediterranean, as does the famous fish market. There, big salmon are thrown through the air to delight the onlookers. One fish nearly clocked one unobservant passerby (cell phoning). Another salmon slammed into the shrieking crowd. The fish turned out to be only a cod, i.e., a stuffed toy. Ah, the old ones are the best—jokes, not fish. Of course, 100 other shops of every description also entertain the window shopper in the Pine Street Market, located beside a pleasant park where buskers compete to peak the interest of lazing onlookers. I suspect I lucked out, hitting town on such a bright blue-hued day.

The similarity to another city on a bay, San Francisco (on a clear day) strikes casual onlookers, in a limp-wristed way. The ambience seems much the same. Maybe it's just the smell of marijuana. Like Chicago, Seattle's downtown is covered by free transport. Sweet.

I just jumped off a bus headed to my hotel, after spotting on a ridge above me the climbing spires of an attractive church. Surprise, St. James Catholic Cathedral appropriately reveals itself to this pilgrim. On the lookout for St. Michael medals, I was given gratis one of St. James instead. Still sweeter.

Below the cathedral stands the public library, a modern temple to learning, which could inspire even without its million books. Indeed, the view from it would suffice. I must fly now, however, to rendezvous with three other guys met aboard the train. We've found a hotel room to share for thirty bucks apiece, legitimately, with full fringe benefits—way better than any hostel.

Hemp-smoking aside, the guys are adventurous travelers like myself. I do hope they're not planning any other "trips," especially not one "around the world." They seem okay to me.

---

09 September 08

The Quality Inn displays a delightful smorgasbord for its free breakfast, worth $30 alone. Feeling full and fit, I'm on my way again, after a slightly scary sprint which construction and misdirection at Seattle's train station made necessary. No need to mention my over-staying at the over-stuffing. Arriving later than desired, we joined the lengthy line for boarding, because no one warned us that we needed to start in another queue first. Judas priest!

Yet, lugging all luggage, we did make the correct carriage, and now relax, rolling south to Sacramento. Just below Seattle sat the town of Slaughter, named after its fine Irish founder. The main hotel, civic pride entitled "The Slaughter House." For some reason this establishment failed to prosper, until the town altered its own name to "Auburn." I would have suggested "Quality."

Ah well, welcome to California. Yup, just as you'd expect, I've just been robbed. Dammit, I do feel quite deflated. For only the second time in a lifetime of travel, I've been relieved of sorely needed cash. Bastards, do I look rich? The first time was 25 years ago on a subway train under New York; the second occurs in bright sunshine on the west coast. I don't know whether to be more disappointed in myself or in humanity at large. I should be glad and grateful no violence was involved in either incident. Though robbed by stealth, I knew almost immediately the guilty parties both times, and contemplated violence myself. Unable to prove anything, I had to let the parasitic scum go. Today's case is particularly galling, as the perp made me pretend I didn't know his guilt. Smarmy git. He'll get his.

I thought myself clever, not hiding all funds in one basket. A couple hundred I'd stashed inside my water carrier. This innocuous pouch, I kept casually at my side in the club car. Once targeted by the professional thieves on a cross-country train, a pigeon can do little to defend himself, however. The chink in the chicken wire takes just a little time to weasel into. I wouldn't ordinarily carry this much cash, and won't in future. At least I've learned my lesson early, still stateside, when adjustments may yet be made.

As if this isn't enough of a sickener, I already felt quite ill. Lack of sleep, exercise and fresh air have combined to clobber me. I do hope an opportunity to recoup surfaces soon. Acute vulnerability during these two months of traveling alone, I do feel sharply now.

--- + ---

Detrained and intending to transfer to the Denver service, I find Sacramento a very modern, geometrically designed city. Yet, she manages to display some old world charm. Bless her, as I can use some charm now. Quite how cette grande femme does it, I do not know, but find it simply captivating. Maybe the Catholic cathedral's prominent hosting of the café class on the central square provides the key. The outdoor café tables, comfortable looking in this Mediterranean climate, certainly help.

Local public transport looks very Continental. Electric trolleys provide elegant transportation. Buses also ply straight avenues. Both modes charge cheap fares. Free again would be too much to expect.

The capital caters well to hostelling travelers as well. One of the few International Youth Hostels in America nests in the heart of downtown Sacramento. This very charming clapboard Victorian-gothic mansion mothers her transient brood very proudly. I feel privileged just to view this house, once a home of privilege. The structure is itself such a treasure, I'm surprised civic authorities let it be dedicated to the needs of hobos like me. $28 for a dorm bed. Not bad.

Take a bus to "Old Sacramento," comfortably nestled on the near bank of the Sacramento River, skirting the downtown area. Though a bit touristy, it's well worth a visit. Both the Pony Express and the Trans-Continental Railroad started from there.

Jarring in the pleasant, peaceful surroundings of the state capital is the monument to fallen police officers, beside the capitol building. Viewing the quantity of names on this inspiring memorial rather lowers the quality of life in what otherwise appears a perfect society. Having just been victimized, I already knew that appearance misleading.

--- + ---

An unsettlingly high number of low-lives have climbed aboard this train, including the one who almost certainly robbed me. Seeing his grinning face again, and not knocking out his teeth, grinds my teeth. I do blame myself for letting my guard slip, but a train proffers a nearly perfect environment for pickpockets and swindlers. Buses cater better for travelers in that respect alone.

--- + ---

Cutting through high rugged mountains again, the tracks are accompanied by "snow sheds" and interesting commentary on boom towns and Donner starvation, outlaws and robber barons. The mountains themselves merely mimic yesterday's Cascades. These plain peaks just don't inspire me overly.

From what I could see, the Mormons can keep Utah. The Green River Canyon must be gained before scenery engages. Colorado, on the other hand, calls for a wake-up call. Best vistas so far.

Grand Junction isn't so grand though. Not awake enough, I nearly missed the train out of town. I judge "G.J." nowhere to be left behind. Construction companies used tailings from local uranium mines to build the school and the rehabilitation center, among other structures. That's what I'm told. I do know for certain, only three pawn shops open for business within a block of the station.

That dearth of life proved a gift from God to me. Had I stopped anywhere, the train would have left without me. Halting times on Amtrak strike me as quite arbitrary. After barely pausing for an ice-lolly in the station, I discovered every door closed on the train, save one. Fortunately, the kitchen car had stopped near the station, and a cook stood smoking at the door. Unfortunately, passenger boarding there violates regulations. I never hesitated. The cook did object, but he'd have needed his cleaver to stop me.

Reaching Denver after dark, I found the opposite of Grand Junction, but that's not good either, not for me. Only fancy restaurants surround "Union Station" (yet another). However, as again no one declared a definite departure time, I again engaged in a fruitless gallop around the block.

---

13 September 08

Nebraska looks nice, not near as flat as expected. God, it's good to see real trees again. A hot breakfast may have improved my outlook. Regular dining in the dining car travels outside my budget, but $6.00 for the lowest-priced plate seems almost reasonable. The product definitely looked and tasted reasonable. This could pass for civilized living.

Iowa remains underwater. Record flooding by the Mississippi has submerged whole cities. The state of crops here, never mind homes, breaks this farm boy's heart. Old Man River looks more like a mighty monster, full of vigor and malevolence, looking to devour all, including our train. "Water, water everywhere." Our club car simulates a pleasure craft cruising through calm seas. A waterlogged track bed reduces our speed to a leisurely number of knots. Only the snowy egrets move happily and easily here, soaring and settling as our cruiser cuts through temporary marshes.

While enjoying the maritime illusion, we're four hours late already, so I hope the bridges (back in reality) still hold. I gave my shipmates a verse and chorus of "Charlie on the M.T.A," as Charlie *"could not get off of that train."*

"Did he ever return?"
"No he never returned,
And his fate is still unlearned.
He may ride forever,
'Neath the streets of Boston.
He's the man who never returned."

In this old political campaign song by the Kingston Trio, a real Irish politico promises to get Charlie off the train. Since Chuck is a fictional character, that's a pretty clever campaign promise.

=== + ===

Six hours late arriving in Chicago, I'm two hours delayed leaving. Flash-flood warnings promise more hold ups before Elkhart, two stops away, in the next state.

=== + ===

14 September 08, 7:00 a.m.
Ridiculous. We've not yet reached the first stop, South Bend, Indiana. I should have reached family, and a proper stationary bed,

in Elkhart last night. Now, I'm supposed to be boarding a train headed in the opposite direction. Any good news? When I woke in bright daylight, I jumped to the scary conclusion that I'd skipped my stop. Ha! Not even close.

Hear my advice. Never criss-cross the continent by rail. If lucky enough to coast from coast to coast once, don't push your luck. Moreover, never board without provisions and survival gear. Summer or winter, you may freeze or swelter. Food may not be found even if you're willing to pay the quadrupled price. Drink the water piped on board at your own peril.

Traveling by train in the USA is like suddenly moving to the Third World. Tinpot dictator aside, underdevelopment and misappropriation compel strict restrictions. Galling. However, I've been impressed by the helpfulness of counter staff. They saved me more than once. Blessedly, all spoke excellent English.

I now appreciate American willingness to abandon railcars for cars. I never did reach Elkhart. Abandoning hope after 12 hours of creeping like a slug towards the town, I jumped at the stop before it. South Bend, surprisingly—or not—had not yet seen the Chicago train. Both train and station staff did not recommend re-embarking however, as they expected the train to take seven more hours to reach Chicago. My connection would be missed for sure. The alternative of a commuter train, competing on another set of tracks, was suggested and accepted. My itinerary could be salvaged for $10. The awkward catch (the commuter station's sitting on the far side of town), Amtrak removed by including a taxi service. Applause.

Even more impressive, my niece arrived and insisted on driving me herself. The taxi was crowded. After some hustle and bustle with heavy baggage, I managed to seat myself comfortably on *the Shoreliner*, just in time to hear the announcement: "Due to flooding…" Had my niece not forgotten her cell phone, I could have retrieved a ride immediately. Instead, I had to wait for hours, but was enabled thereby to scalp my ticket, and to aid a damsel, even more distressed than I, in need of a lift.

All my distress worked for the best, as while I waited, Amtrak called to apologize. They offered to push forward my entire itinerary two days—precisely what I preferred. An act of God extended my rail pass two days, to allow me to work on my niece's home while resting from my travels.

--- + ---

What I called an act of God, should more accurately be described as a bureaucratic snafu (easily confused). All while our train crept through the night, freight trains barreled by ("like a freight train") often forcing our service into sidings. The problem is that the commercial companies own the tracks and dictate their use. So, whenever the freight carrier can deem the track bed soggy, snowy or whatever, Amtrak can be ordered not to exceed 15 m.p.h. If Amtrak fails to comply, the freight shleppers can be absolved of all responsibility for proper track maintenance. In theory, for all the government assistance to railroads, passengers take priority over commodities. Loopholes in the law are easily obtained however. Taxpayers have no real lobby. As a result of "emergency exemptions," freight rules the rails.

--- + ---

17 September 08

Not only are passenger trains railroaded, passengers aboard a train can be railroaded to make life easier for conductors. Sometimes conductors arbitrarily assign seats. A passenger can be forced to sit next to someone with obvious health issues (mental or physical) though half the carriage is empty. Conductors make judgments like Joe Stalin. Finally, after a bad night, I was allowed to move, one stop prior to my strange seat partner's departure. Most of the night I'd already passed in the club car, with cards and chess.

However, if not for my forced exile, I might not have met the woman I call Elena. She lost to me at chess, but beat me in the game of hearts, an excellent card game. She is the first outside the family to buy my book. Had I more copies, more could have been sold. A dozen friendships I cobbled in the club car. A few may reach beyond these rails.

Had an hour to wait in Albuquerque, New Mexico. This city assures us that the wide open spaces of the West have been reached. Finding food meant quite the run. I arrived back aboard, however, without incident (and with grub). The unnecessary sprawl of urban America must have originated out here where room seems limitless. Even the architecture of the average American strip mall looks like it owes much to the ranch and Spanish mission architectural styles of the southwest.

---

18 September 08

Rousted but not roasted by the cops in Williams, Arizona, I must leave this "gateway to the Grand Canyon." Arriving late, knowing I would leave early, made a public bench an attractive choice for a few hours of rest. The bench I picked was a bit *too* public, and *too* private property. The bus to the canyon was cornered and caught within a half hour. In fact, breakfast, toilet break, and water re-supply, plus the cheapest way to the canyon ($22), were all located and lassoed in under that time. Yippee-ki-yea!

Not so nice, graffiti carved into the picnic table at my otherwise excellent, legal campsite ($6 fee; entry fee $6) in the Grand

Canyon National Park reads: "Fuck Big Fat Americans. Respect the nature. Eat less. Walk more. Drive less. Think more."

Ya, but what excuses have Europeans for their increasing obesity, and race-rioting? They have the American example of the wrong way to go, and go down that road regardless. Think about that.

More French is overheard here than English. No need for me to check the euro exchange rate. I like to hear "La plus belle langue." Not so nice to hear "Cochon" repeated. The landscape is too large for me to be small though.

---

19 September 08

Am I scared? You bet your ass, and jackasses are very valuable in the Grand Canyon. I have only shank's mare for a long hot run to the bottom and back today. Warned ten times by experts never to attempt this feat, I'm doing it anyway, having neither time nor money to do otherwise. If only 1 percent of the four million annual visitors descend all the way, how many go down and up in a day?

The Canyon kills, but altitude sickness seems the real culprit in this 20-mile hike. Of course, some other sickness must be involved in this dramatic masochistic binge, but the altitude (not attitude) illness surprises. Most visitors travel suddenly from the desert floor to 7,000 feet above sea level, at the canyon rim. On this high plateau, due to the flatness, the oxygen-light altitude is not perceived. After jumping one mile down, by a 10-mile route, the body will protest when pressed into the altered pressure of the return climb.

Last night provided little rest besides. Aside from cold and cramps, the coyote calls and cougar reports kept my slumber skittish. Rising before light at 4:15, I should be running now, not writing. In my insomnia, the notion occurred to me to make a rattle (gravel in plastic bottle). By rattling around the tents of my fellow campers, I could share my insomnia. However, I reckon this is no time to gather bad karma.

Moonlight floods the campsite, producing deep shadows besides hoary half-light from the earth. Not frost, but a phosphorescent dust reflects light. Slightly spooky.

Finding the toilet block closed, I went in desperate search of another. One hour before sunrise, crows begin their cacophony at first light. By 5:45 the rooks raucously rebuke me for remaining in a camp I ought to have fled an hour ago.

--- + ---

Caught the bus (to the trailhead), only to have it go out of service. Damn. No time to pull up stakes. Tent and belongings I left to the mercy of authorities and thieves, only adding to my stress. My most essential gear, except for immediate survival, I deposited in the nearest hotel baggage office.

--- + ---

7:15 a.m., starting down Kaibob Trail, a half-hour after sunrise. I forgot sun block in my rush. Should have changed to shorts. Glad I didn't now. A canyon sunrise will still be viewed below. "Kelly the Boy from Killan" breaks out once more, an Irish rebel tune to rouse any spirit but an Englishman's. Yahooing as I run into the canyon, I should be conserving energy, but my adrenalin glands pump madly. That's the way my body works. We'll be sorry later, but for now I am adrenalin-drunk and singing.

Having pushed ahead of the early-start crowd, I'm rewarded by squirrels and lizards scurrying, and peaceful rest stops for me. Toilet closed.

Sun lotion borrowed, I've rolled my pant-legs. The heavy dust should protect my shin bones anyway, except from the yellow rattlers (unique to here). Better stay on the path if I don't want to be struck by "lightning." Green rattlers in the Mojave are reputably even meaner, more aggressive.

8:15 a.m., almost five miles. First water break. No water source on the Kaibob before the Colorado.

Just a half-hour later, resting in very cool shade, I enjoy more water. Bypassing a mule train and every hiker in view, I remind all that, "Jackasses do have the legal right-of-way on canyon trails!" I'm an Irish jackass with blinding shin bones, and green shit besides. The piles mules leave look florescent green. Copper in the drinking water?

9:00 a.m., a blooming cactus reminds me to water myself again. Greenness surprises here. Record annual rainfall explains some verdant hues, even in the fall, but copper ore colors more. Even squirrels go greenish here, and dusty hikers gain extra "green around the gills" paleness. All other colors in the canyon look as autumnal and breathtaking as expected.

Nearly to the Colorado, I hear a mule train striking its tattoo upon the bridge below. Soon they will be crowding me on this narrow, winding, dusty path. They're making messy booby-traps for me now.

I can spy them emerging from a tunnel, perhaps the mouth of hell, as the tormenting heat suggests.

The tunnel attained, comparative coolness reminds more of a monastic cloister. *Agnus Dei* grabs a good echo effect. My prayers are answered. Of all who left the rim after sunrise, I reach the river first.

At the storied Phantom Ranch I bought a souvenir hiking stick, and a postcard for the Mule Mail. Having addressed to myself a message from an Irish folksong, "Are you right there, Michael?" I hope I live to read that note. I'm headed the long way around the world, to meet the mailman.

Pink Vishnu schist from the floor of the Grand Canyon makes a better souvenir. As the hand of man continues to hamper and control the Colorado, I lend a hand to the river, carrying away a few pebbles myself. It's only fair, after cooling my feet in Bright Angel Creek. We'll bring some fool's gold too, appropriately promised to a particular friend, a bright angel. Bright Angel Trail beckons to me, cleverly promising water along its length.

--- + ---

11:00 a.m., first over Silver Bridge, my ascent begins. The river raves below, a raging beige! A sign orders: "No swimming." No kidding. If you need that advice, you're too stupid to read.

After my efforts to charge my phone, no service works its way down here. I could need help out of this hole. So far, so good though. Warned of temperatures above 100°F, I don't feel too bad yet. To what the thermometer reads above, tack on 25 below. Even the notorious "Box" hasn't suffocated me.

--- + ---

Uh, oh, spoke too soon. Puking already. I shoulda stopped at Phantom Ranch to eat and rest. Indian Gardens, the next rest area, waits far too far away (and high up) to reach readily. On the map, in theory, the Gardens should be an easy row to hoe. Big mistake. As I search for shade, a circling condor looks for a late lunch.

--- + ---

1:30 p.m., arrived at Indian Gardens to enjoy cold water, and the famous floorshow from cheeky squirrels. I swear these rodents put on a variety act in front of the benches, while their relatives rob the pack on your back. Remember also that squirrel bites lead to more infirmary visits than any other cause.

2:15 p.m., leaving. Four and a half miles hard climbing to go.

North America's largest bird, the California Condor, lands on the ledge above me; hummingbirds meanwhile whirl beside me. Other colorful songbirds, strangers to me, try to cheer me along in my ordeal.

After the last water-point, I am not seeing much more than the dust at my feet. Remember man that you are dust. Every second switchback demands a halt for cramp massaging and gut wrenching.

Ten of those pit-of-my-stomach stops took me to the top of the trail. Still standing, I staggered to the nearest bus stop, and to what should be the final showing of my dramatic "Black Bile Follies."

━━ ✠ ━━

By divine intervention, a new bus schedule delivers a conveyance in time to bring me to the bus rendezvousing with the train in Flagstaff. Both the driver and I are anxious to be off, but I must first beg for delay, for the driver to swing by the campsite and hotel for my gear, while he worries about another extra pick up in Williams for the train. The consideration of this stranger, during my greatest need, amounts to a miracle.

At the campground the Horned One sent a herd of elk, with antlers like rocking chairs, to interfere. With no hesitation, I bolted through that camp to rip my tent from the ground, and to sprint through the hotel, lugging my body weight in bulky baggage. The impatient busman was impressed by a corpse's liveliness.

Still, the train passenger waiting in Williams did concern, until he turned out to be me! Two places at once! How's that for impressive? Don't ask how that happened. I don't know. What's more, this bus company, substituting for another, thought they owed me a refund. Though they must be mistaken, I'm too dazed and grateful to argue. They should have surcharged me, for heaving more than my luggage on their bus. I did manage to keep it all in a plastic bag.

---+---

As the train arrived a little late, I had time to change my sweat-soaked clothes in the station loo, while boking some more. Without a ticket, nausea boarded the train with me.

Imagine my chagrin then, after another race to the cubicle, at finding two liters of expensive, pure Fiji water (long carried) discarded by careless car attendants. Admitting their incompetence, staff pledged replacement. Expecting only two small bottles of purified water, I vowed not to complain. When nothing came, in desperation, I did complain, producing one tiny eight-ounce bottle much later.

The irresponsible response, of people responsible for the culprit responsible for discarding the water of a dangerously dehydrated man, further drained that dry guy. The official response repeated that the passenger alone must take total responsibility for anything brought aboard. So, no passenger may sleep or pee during trans-continental travel as railroad staff are licensed to steal or destroy anything not Amtrak property. Indeed, they can do that in your face. Ordinary hooligans also seem to operate with impunity, but with much less brass.

Whatever happens to your stuff, Amtrak staff (top to bottom) cannot be held responsible. No, I guess not. No need to say more.

---+---

20 September 08

Still alive. That was easily the hardest deed I've ever done. The good news? My personal constitution must have been born better than ever I imagined. Though I should be dead, I would not be afraid to try hiking again the Grand Canyon in a day—just not today. The added pressure of a departure deadline should be avoided though. That would remove the campsite checkout as well. At 5 o'clock, a.m. or p.m., the fewer worries the better. I'd acclimatize for a day at least on the canyon rim if possible. Best to locate previously the 24-hour toilet too. Then, you may just walk out of the campground on time, 5:00 a.m., in time to snag the first bus to the Kaibob trailhead.

Go ahead then, run down if you like, if the light is good, but don't waste energy as I did. Rein in, if you would reign yourself, and rule the day, not rue it. You'll rest at the ranch before 8:00 a.m. After breakfast, turn around by 9:00 a.m. Two hours more will put you in shade on the Bright Angel Trail. Rest. Let your body adjust for two hours. At 1:00 or 2:00 p.m. move out, but take ten whenever you find shade, and keep taking H2O. You'll be out before 5:00 (when shade prevails), an hour before the Flagstaff bus. Wiser you'd be, to bus only to your tent and bedroll, and to that grandest of deep chasms: sleep.

L.A.'s Union Station, Moorish/Mission architecture on a grand scale, suggests a movie set, and today it is. Though this station appears nearly as grand as Grand Central, Los Angeles presents the ugliest urban landscape I've ever seen when exiting (headed south).

San Diego seems comparatively civilized, remarkably so, considering its border-town status. A virtually free city trolley operates regularly to the Mexican border and back. ($5 day passes bus/rail go unchecked.) I never realized Tijuana trafficked so closely with San Diego.

The U.S. city's premier tourist attraction could possibly be the Cabrillo National Monument, part of a U.S. Navy base. Stellar views delight the eyes, whenever the Navy permits. Tourist info should warn that the park closes at 5:00 p.m., before the final bus there. Private security firms turn tourists away. Oddly, the shore patrol doesn't guard either navy base in town. How weird is that? The government grants contracts to private firms to guard our military bases? These guys are obviously ex-military, snappily professional. Are mercs hired to distance the government from any liabilities or casualties? What is going on?

"Old Town" was recommended to me, but I won't do that to you. Maybe going later improves it. A highlight of my day, finding (en route to Old Town) a Trader Joe's (best grocer in the universe), should have put me in a better mood. We'll not bore with details. Let's just describe the Trader's as a health food supermarket.

--- + ---

L.A., Sunday, 21 September 08

In time for Mass, I found the massive Cathedral of Our Lady, Queen of Angels, despite the edifice looking more like a faceless corporate headquarters. Unaffectionately called "the Concrete Armadillo," the church displays startlingly modern architecture, built genuinely recently. That the Church could afford such an undertaking in our times surprises most. That seemed particularly so when the pews stood empty of sitters. However, if the Irish famously streel late into Mass, Latinos show later, and Chinese come last. Perhaps parishioners gamble with their souls on missing the collection without missing Mass mortally. Pews had grown groaningly full by the offertory. The Chinese do famously gamble fanatically.

Plenty of room waits downstairs though—in the mausoleum. Space for the departed apparently sells to shelter the living above. Gregory Peck, a late Irish-American, was recently interred down there.

Appropriately for your peregrino de Santiago, an ancient altarpiece from Spain, dedicated to St. James, decorates the main entry way. My pilgrim staff from the Phantom Ranch received baptism in water and the Holy Spirit there.

=== + ===

San Diego

My trusty companion also took baptism in the Pacific Ocean near San Diego. I'm back on a mission. Already I successfully obtained a bed in a party-hard hostel on the beach. No, I'm not partying, but surely one night and morning on a beach in Southern Cal must be a prerequisite of this trip.

Unexpectedly, the hostel is full of Irish people, and other Europeans—not of migrant Mexicans. The bayside of Mission Bay seems also unnaturally quiet. No wave or person waves there. On the ocean side, only waves move, until you reach the decking of the animal house where I am supposed to sleep.

=== + ===

22 September 08

Well, I did sleep quite well, thank you. All the animals proved rather thoughtful and engaging, even when fogged in alcohol. They're in sharp contrast to Southern Californians who are rude and recalcitrant as a rule, far worse than New Yorkers. My new friends seem even deferential to my age. Some young ladies, you might consider too friendly. Young women really should steer clear of alcohol. No more effective birth/disease control than sobriety exists. Binge drinking, accompanied by smoking, wreaks havoc in the western world among young women more than males now.

As I did not indulge, or take advantage, I woke this morning in time for a stroll on the beach, sure cure for every ill, from planter's warts to fuzzy brains. Nope, only a slap-up breakfast at IHOP defeated hunger pains. All personal pain mollified, the public problem of a $700,000,000,000 debt continues to hurt. If that does not say, "Hard times a-comin'," what does? Looks like we're walking on the cusp of a volcano. Am I traveling in the nick of time? Sure do hope so. Breakfasted, I'm breaking fast for the border now, but not before seeing what I missed last time, the Cabrillo.

=== + ===

The Cabrillo peninsula must embrace the most impressive military cemetery in the country. Views of the Pacific and San Diego, city and bay, port and airport (commercial and military) impress the hell out of the living and the dead.

The past impresses equally with the present. Juan Cabrillo, first European to land here (1542) earned his immortality by dying here only 50 years after Columbus located Central America's east coast. This captain, one-time corporal, constructed a fleet of European ships on the western coast, before sailing to Alta California and his fate. (Of all the great conquistadores, only Cortes returned with wealth to die in bed in Spain.)

=== + ===

Crossing the border, I'm first reminded of an old Amish couple met on the train. A wide-open border town in Mexico ought not to suggest staid folk from the heartland. However, I learned on the train that Amish families travel across country, and over the border, to find affordable healthcare. An entire plaza of medical, dental and pharmaceutical providers confronts every visitor to Mexico immediately, and should affront every American. Though these services must be dubious at best, as many Americans must use them, all Americans (not Mexicans) should be ashamed.

All other shops require hawkers at their doors, waiting to swoop on the unsuspecting. All goods (from many foods to rosaries), plus many "bads" (gambling to sex), sell openly. With effort, I managed to escape without being hustled, and without being poisoned (as I ate nothin'). One ring was purchased at a fair price for a fair lady, far away. As darkness fell, I literally ran for the border. I wouldn't want to be found in Tijuana after dark. If ever you're similarly hurrying, do expect chaos at customs though. Presenting an American passport presents no advantage there.

Into this Third World disorder, the New World Order would have all America descend.

I grow more sympathetic to the unfriendly Californians. A whole lot of weirdoes wander on the loose here. That comes from someone who likes to think of himself as odd. This is what you get for accepting license instead of freedom: poverty and insanity. A patently psychopathic vagrant rode the trolley with me to Tijuana. Judging by the incoherent threats muttered all the way to Mexico, he had only recently been released from custody somewhere. Little use that incarceration served.

Prisons really should be abandoned in the USA. Boot camps and community service certainly are needed, but *not* expensive prisons producing zero rehabilitation. Insane asylums, for the protection of lunatics, as well as society's saner members, must continue to operate—as humanely as humanly possible. The specimen opposite me on the trolley had no business being out in public. Such insane individuals must be locked up, or no individual can hold any rights. If society does not protect us from lunacy (which most anti-social behavior is) all individuals live under tyranny, a constant threat of chaos.

Prisons, however, fail to protect society. While costing that society billions, they cost individuals incarcerated more. Damaged or destroyed persons, prisons then release upon society to inflict further loss. Our nation needs *more* control than prisons can provide. Total license constitutes the opposite of freedom. This oppression, not by society or majorities, but by minorities and individuals, is the law of the jungle. The average citizen, currently unable to control his own environment (or protect the natural environment), is instead subjected to the whims of whoever grows loudest, wildest, rudest or richest.

The right to privacy should mean precisely that, not publicity. No one holds a right to invade the personal space of anyone else. Those screaming loudest about such invasion tend to be guiltiest of it: the media, most "liberals," maybe most young people, all the truly intolerant politically correct. My empathy with hard-pressed Californians stops short, however, at shockingly rampant racism, casually displayed.

Back in San Diego, still on public transport, a raging alcoholic decided to introduce himself. Returning from a counseling program he was legally obliged to attend, the indigent gent vented on me. Fortunately I wasn't the target of his venom, just of the spittle sprayed (even before the coughing fit). Though he tried to cover his mouth, I let my hat double as shower cap. By God's mercy, my interlocutor's stop appeared shortly, but rising to leave, this well-met fellow extended his hand for a hearty shake.

My stop would be ignored by the driver. Being dropped one stop too far meant missing my return bus. That could have cost me the connection to a bus to the train in L.A. Making my connection on the run, I left behind my favorite staff.

Wee hours of 23 September 08

Having caught the bus to L.A. alright, I went somewhere else. Yup, I fell asleep, as one does on late-night buses, and woke two hours past my stop, headed for Bakersfield. Having been aboard the bus-train to Union Station, I had no reason to fear missing my stop. No way would it happen on any bus into New York City. However, anxious hours and luggage hassle aside, my new itinerary serves me better. Nearly the schedule I had sought (and been denied), I needed to find it myself by accident.

Obviously, rail service in America rolls in terminal condition to its terminals. Noting bullet trains in Europe and Asia, Americans gain another cause for embarrassment. I'm not saying no one should set foot on Amtrak trains. Au contraire, do it while you can. If you have all the time in the world, and no time for worldly possessions, you'll probably have a grand time.

Want another American disgrace? No foreign exchanges anywhere. Every hotel in Europe, and most stores, can provide this service. Here, even most bankers choke on it. Forget about post offices.

Sacramento 23 September 08

"Transiberian," the movie viewed in the venerable Crest Theatre, provided a useful cautionary tale for me, en route to the Transiberian. Not brilliant cinema, it may just save my life. Anyway, holding a ticket for the real Transiberian Railroad, I was granted a discount on the movie ticket, very kindly.

Feast Day of St. Michael, 29 September 08

Even kinder were cousins in three locations between Sacramento and San Francisco. How nice to connect with kin before departing the country, nice despite mushroom poisoning and intestinal flu. I can't afford to worry about all that, even if I had the time.

Reaching out to a niece not near at hand, Michaela back in Indiana, I institute today the Order of St. Michael, to honor all who bravely fight the good fight.

In honor of Michaelmas Night, I entertained the entire club car with "The Spalpeen's Lament."

I well recollect it was Michaelmas Night.
To a fine hearty supper he did me invite:
One cup of sour milk, that was more green than white.
And it gave me the trotting disorder.

My unfortunate intestines, more than the date, may have summoned to mind that song.

Outside, beauty distracts me from my ugly insides: Avila Beach, Morro Bay, San Luis Obispo. After breathing here, if I can only reach Warsaw in Poland, I will die happily. To keel over anywhere more blissfully, I'll need to return to a "Warsaw Road" in upstate New York, in time for Thanksgiving, and still able to eat.

Maybe none of us will make it home for Thanksgiving. Recognizing that we have passed the Age of Faith to enter the endtime of prophesy fulfilled, I see the evidence surrounding us everywhere. The great game reaches end-game. Sides must be selected now. May the way of God be clear to you.

Climbing out of San Luis, the train sweeps slowly and cruelly past the state pen. Negotiating painstakingly the biggest horseshoe bend in the country produces views of the entire train, to passengers and escaped cons alike. I'm reminded of my own soul's curious journey.

--- + ---

San Fran, 30 September 08

They say you can never go back. Disappointment forms a formidable obstacle. Today, Svenson's Ice Cream Parlor failed to delight. However, everywhere San Francisco's other treasures beckon. From around corners, narrow streets cresting hills call me to high bridges or low waterfront. Every opening finds a view fit for a viewfinder. Today, when sunlight highlights any angle, I could snap pix all day, if I only owned a camera. I can write descriptions to encourage others to come, to view for themselves this beautiful burg on the bay. Come before it's too late.

Even Alcatraz cannot look grim and cold on a day such as this. Today I've looked at that island from every angle but from on it. Okay, not from the trajectory of para-surfing kite sailors. They float and flit beneath the Golden Gate, flouting the laws of gravity and common sense. As all para-sports suggest paraplegia, I'll pass, but watching entertains safely. I'll also pass on the devil's island they play around. Dwelling on evil, even only in the mind, does not dwell well with my soul.

Views in San Francisco are greatly enhanced by the absence of obesity. However, the not-so-beautiful people would be the hundreds of hobos everywhere.

Nearly a hobo myself, I chose my cheap accommodation badly. I picked a downtown hostel where construction restricted movement at night, and woke us all before daylight. That's not right, and not funny. Neither was the shower, though laughable. I'll not name names as that might disservice you. The construction may have left this location better than the alternatives by now. My suggestion is *not* to book early in San Francisco's case, as accommodation abounds. Ask around, on the internet at least.

If you want to see something hilarious, imagine me running for the airport train which would then sit a half-hour before I gave up. Escaping to a taxi with other stranded strap-hangers, I still managed to reach the airport in time (even to sell my rapid transit ticket). The anxiety crowding into that taxi barely left room for four passengers with luggage. In my case, the stalled train followed a rushed visit to the internet in a public library, after a trolley and a trot to a bank (while fully loaded myself).

All the while, intestines and sinuses ran fast enough to keep a sane man in bed. I belong in bedlam. After a month of meeting strangers unscathed on the train, I succumb when finally stopped, and before enplaning for China, and a whole new world of contagion.

CHAPTER 2

Asia

Hong Kong, 2 October 08, a post-dateline Thursday

If you follow me, keep a sharp eye peeled for the tourist info booth, inside the restricted arrivals area—just prior to baggage reclaim and customs (which require a train to attain). Once in the Great Hall, where you would expect to look, you're too late. Following "*i*" signs then, produces useless computer screens only. I opt for the shuttle bus serving all hotels, though I might be "taken for a ride" at $20 (US).

Never mind, free luggage trolleys were provided at the airport—a true sign of a civilized country. However, the weather stays warm and muggy in October, and as smoggy as feared. After ten hours flying under a heavy flu, I'm ready to retire for the night (whatever the cost) to my booked hotel, the Evergreen.

Having taken the shuttle bus, I must say the $20 seems a bargain. Along the long route, the city still jumps, long after 10 p.m. She calls like a siren to me, but I do fear crashing on the rocks. Here goes.

※ ✦ ※

3 October 08

Yes, full of bazaar, the streets defeated common sense. Yes, I also have bought something for someone I ought not to have. She came to my mind, far from home, when a trinket I spied, and blink, I had plunked down the price. Common sense loses again.

Nevertheless, I laid in bed quite early (thinking of her), and I rose early with an appetite. Call me a foreign fool if you like, I call an Asian breakfast one odd beast.

Free internet in the train station provides another very civilized feature, but, outside in an acid rain, the city reminds me of a "Blade-runner" set.

Naturally my arrival coincides with a typhoon's. Also naturally, I determined to take the famous cable cars anyway, without a notion of how far the cables extend. Not too long I hope, time-wise at least, as I must meet my fellow travelers this evening.

Sure 'nuff, my cable car stops dead, 200 feet above the bay, with the wind picking up. Hong Kong's Disneyland couldn't top this. The cliff-face cemetery passed en route looked pretty scary though. Huge expanses of Hong Kong appear remarkably desolate. Scrub-covered mountains now wait below my climbing car.

My objective, the Big Buddha, hunkers down on a mountain top, granting himself a grand view, well worth the price I paid. The bronze behemoth sits serenely, despite the slightly jarring swastika tattooed on his chest. I should mention that the symbol long pre-dated the Nazis, and the current peace symbol, as did the prophesy of a peaceful third reich.

One word of warning, I had decided not to take the cable car, and not to climb the long stair to the Buddha's seventh heaven. The steps to the cable car depot were meant to suffice, but my pilgrim feet took over. Having seen and done everything else, I elected to take the cheaper option back down ($17.50 H.K.) because the line for the bus-line looked closer and shorter. The packed transport also turned out slower and scarier. The coach careens down a one-lane road, with two-way traffic. Occasionally, the ramshackle vehicle plows through oddly Spanish villages full of cattle and Chinese people.

An hour later, still alive, I arrived at the Stanford Hotel, and managed to catch up with my tour group in a nearby restaurant. Just three other travelers, all Aussies, and a pretty, petite Mongol guide make-up the group. Harroo-hooray, I promised all a shot of Irish whiskey for my being late, and for my birthday. That penance and celebration I will not be able to deliver however. The convenience store, 7-11, does sell whiskey here, very conveniently, but it's all scotch! I'm shocked. Further search proved futile.

I wish to commend Sundowner Tours for their willingness to deliver a tour for this few people. We garner all advantages of a big tour, without the disadvantages. This few may turn out too few though.

As the stress of travel builds among four strangers accustomed to independent travel, pressure may blow the lid. The nature of larger groups supplies release valves lacking here. Judging by our first hotel's comfortable quality level, we may not require any pressure valves however.

--- + ---

04 October 08

Chen Clan Temple, in Guang Zhou City (old Canton), where this clan's ancestors have long been worshiped, now stands open as a museum and school. Exquisite carving, inside and out, in every material and color, brick to ivory, astonishes, and curiously calms the viewer's soul.

Some new temples in Canton impress even more: the glass sky-scraping temples to the new god, Materialism. State sponsored capitalism has created a new city in two decades, beside the ancient crumbling one.

Commerce also thrives in the elder locality, where we visited an ancient, and current, market for Chinese medicine. 1000 vendors sell similar varieties of animal, vegetable, mineral—common and exotic—to cure every ill.

Whatever your malady, you probably contracted it in a public loo, diabolical in mainland China. The stench inside the train station W.C. overpowers. Outside, you may want to hold your breath, even while hauling luggage up steep steps to the platform. All the other shit in the air worsens as we go inland.

What happened to the Herculean clean-up for the Olympics? Choosing to come now was very deliberately determined by me. Yet, few folks wear masks, and I've not seen masks for sale. Those who do cover their faces have flu already, and are encouraged to keep their germs patriotically to themselves. Our little tour group does feel under attack, as all develop coughs.

Though prior inoculation for cholera, yellow fever, hepatitis, tetanus and typhus come officially recommended, not required, I took no shots, as I could not afford any, and doubted their effectiveness and safety anyway.

--- + ---

Toilets aboard trains remain locked for 15 minutes on either side of all stations. The sign posted on the toilet doors summarized my status better than the loo's: *"No occupation while stabilizing."* Consider that an alternative title to this book.

--- + ---

Our tour group declares unanimously: pre-arranging a guide for China was wonderfully wise. Negotiating train travel demands—scheduling and ticketing, platform and taxi organizing—demand the full-time attention of an experienced, paid professional. Our guide, unable to list Chinese among her four fluent languages, in fact employs many professionals to smooth and explain our path.

Being a foreigner here herself makes her successful results the more impressive. I look forward to studying in Mongolia the society which produced this remarkable young woman, a professional guide and law student, as intellectually lively as she is physically lovely.

5 October 08

Four-star hotels! I'm quite unaccustomed to traveling at this level, even loath to do so generally, but I feared traveling at any lower level in China. Official International Youth Hostels do abound here though, and seem clean and respectable. On this tour however, I receive great bang for my buck in my grand accommodations. Yet, since entering China, I have been entered by athlete's foot, verucas, sore-leg syndrome (muscles overworked in bad air), and Irritable Bowel Syndrome (an explosively gaseous gut). Other afflictions—falling hair, failing eyes, aching head, paining teeth—may have been brought from the USA, but do not improve in China.

Yet, while watching cultural performances from various Chinese dynasties, I indulged in the included fare: a cultural culinary display. I nearly overthrew my constitution by dabbling in dangerous dumplings. Diabolically glutinous creations, they ought to be avoided at all times, at all cost. To sample so many varieties begged for difficulties. At least one of these labor intensive little pastries bit into me.

The Qin (chin) dynasty unified and named China, by constructing a wall, and dictating one tongue. This admirable order fell into chaos with the death of the emperor in 210 B.C. The peasants revolted under the burden of the imperial mausoleum. They nearly destroyed it and all memory of it.

Near Xian (shin), an ancient capital of China, can be found an imperial army formed of clay. (Aren't we all?) 10,000 terracotta warriors and horses were buried here, to guard the dead so grandiosely that the living felt compelled to destroy, despite having created the clay figures with their own sweat and blood. Lost in time, the remaining complex was discovered by a peasant digging a well in 1974.

The shaft nearly missed its mystery mark, the eighth Wonder of the World. You can't miss, and shouldn't miss, the sprawling new complex constructed above the old. I could even have had the humble discoverer sign a book about it, and do regret not having done so.

I did visit a factory replicating and retailing terracotta warriors, along with other works by traditional artisans—but I purchased nothing. Even more interesting, a silk factory provided another missed opportunity to purchase silk guaranteed genuine. Back in my hotel room, most remarkably of all, I was able to view freely on TV from the far side of the world, the destruction of my own civilization. Like all other oppressive empires, it is fated to fall under the overweening greed of the usurpers of power.

--- + ---

Tuesday 7 October 08

Rain. Rain I will always remember most about Xian. The city's ancient ramparts tramped, and the historic bell tower climbed, I more practically visited a post office, a food store, and a restaurant during the day, all in a downpour. The grocery grew into the most interesting stop. An upscale version of a Marks & Sparks food hall (an oriental Harrods perhaps), this establishment proudly displays prices too pricey for me. This shop caters to the Chinese bourgeoisie. No visible difference could you discern between this "communist" society and the capitalist west, except for fewer failures.

Wednesday 8 October 08, 4:00 a.m.

Usually, with dysentery, you feel better after crapping. Not this time. The worst is I can't guess what was consumed to produce this pain. Something has stuck its claws into my gut, and refuses to let go.

My difficulties may not even be caused by something ingested. Attempting to do a nice thing, I began to purchase a souvenir, a Chinese musical instrument, from a very talented vendor, for my more talented brother. Following instruction, I blew into the traditional, egg-shaped instrument of clay. Rather than sweet notes striking my ears, black dust hit my eyes and nose. God only knows what that did to me. Maybe nothing at all. The culprit could be the shower water. A waiter or shop assistant may have served up hepatitis, or anything equally dread. If I seek medical care, I may face even more dangerous invasions, or an evacuation which would cost me my trip, and maybe much more. It could save my life, on the other hand. While I can still stand, I'm not stopping.

10:30 a.m.

Taxis in Beijing seem extremely reasonable and plentiful. Off we go to Tiananmen Square (where else?). Alleged the largest in the world, this plaza stretches forth from the Forbidden City, and includes the Tomb of Mao. Atmospheric of St. Peter's Square in Rome, this extraordinary pilgrimage site cannot elicit the same feeling from this tourist. Chinese pilgrims look enthused though.

China is measured from Tiananmen Square. The center of the universe is the Temple of Heaven, however, a World Heritage Site. The Temple of Good Harvest, located in that temple complex, is a piece or peace of architecture, perfectly constructed all of wood, without a nail. The Lama Temple holds the world's largest wooden carving: a standing Buddha, all of a piece, listed in the Guinness Book of Records.

Go. The odd thing though? The sense of sacred is missing here. Such is the power of communism.

The neighboring district is called a hutong: ordinary homes, traditionally designed and constructed along narrow alleys. Little of this old style remains in Beijing. More destructive than Mao's Cultural Revolution, the new capitalist revolution operates with even less human feeling.

Thursday 9 October 08

My stick from the floor of the Grand Canyon has now climbed to the top of China's Great Wall. Yes, I did buy the t-shirt. I also tried to throw our Mongol guide off the wall. Despite that, she took us to the crypt of the Ming Dynasty's Mausoleum. The structure above cleverly employs the entire landscape.

No way would I have come close to viewing what I have in China, or seeing it as fully, without our Mongol guide. The high point of her efforts I identify as the Chinese acrobats show. A dozen girls waving feathery fans from one bicycle appealed most to me, but the guys did more death-defying stunts. En route, the new modern buildings could be described as even more death defying. Spectacular too. And fun. The Media Center Building portrays the Olympic Torch, and displays the largest TV screen ever seen.

The architects are either brilliantly bright or drunkenly stupid. They could be drunk on power as Western architects are offered carte blanche here. The various human costs affecting western projects go unconsidered.

Friday, 10 October 08, 8:45 a.m.

The Forbidden City, surprisingly not "on the tour," was left to me on a "free day." Of all the wonders found there, two natural ones impressed me most. The largest stone carving from a single block that I have ever seen appears nearly as long and wide as Wednesday's wood carving. Multitudes dragged the block on iced roads to Beijing (Peking) in the 15th century.

Four-hundred-year-old trees shading me in the Imperial Garden make me their favorite. Artifice places in the Garden "The Hill of Accumulated Elegance," where "a single act of carelessness leads to the eternal loss of beauty." Still, surely I'm not forbidden to bring a tiny fallen blossom to a flower not fallen.

Among palaces I prefer the Palace of Mental Cultivation, where Sir Reginald Johnston (Sir Peter O'Toole on film) tutored "The Last Emperor." The best throne room, built under the north wall, is how I describe an empty public restroom.

--- + ---

The Olympic Complex proved very complex. After the Forbidden City (a complex of palaces built for the emperor alone), a complex constructed for the common people refreshes one person's psyche. After a walk through, I taxied to one of the premier public parks on the planet, the Summer Palace, also created for the emperor only. Views of, and from, his private chapel are particularly breathtaking, though just climbing the stairs to there could cause that effect.

At least I couldn't blame the smog, as the weather had turned perfect for touring: bright and clear, not too hot, for two days. Our guide declares having never seen two such days in Beijing before.

To picture the Summer Palace, imagine Central Park in New York being owned by the Rockefeller family, before being confiscated for the public. Coincidently, most of this contrived creation is no older than Central Park's public works. English and French forces destroyed everything in the late 19th century just to convince the emperor that he could not stop them. The royal reaction was to misappropriate funds from the military budget to rebuild the imperial pleasure garden, almost appropriately—in a warped way. The navy funds did provide a stone ship on the large lake.

Incidentally, loads of Chinese folks vied to take photos with me. Strange. Foreign tourists remain foreign to most Chinese natives, and our genetic difference is truly striking, however small it must be. Even stranger, the snap-happy natives ignored a vibrant blond Hungarian woman (with me by fluke). Ha! Apparently, blonds are thought, by the unanimously raven-haired Chinese, as too freakish to be beautiful, as a westerner might consider an albino. My white hair deserved respect as a badge of age. Age still calls for respect in Eastern cultures.

I do believe my blond acquaintance was a little put out at the attention given me, though relieved at the same time.

Time pressure, created by the nearly commanded leisure of the impressive imperial park, pushed me into an unofficial taxi, which did take me for a bit of a ride. Watch out for that.

The most exciting sightseeing for me came after, when wandering on my own through darkened streets, among the ordinary people. Though not feeling threatened there, even in a warren of shops in a hutong district, I did feel most alone and most alive there, bargaining for souvenirs of my fond memory. Once, where workmen blocked the lane, I needed to navigate down a narrow back-alley, or dirt track, in black of night. Though relieved to leave there, I did sail through without a wreck.

Saturday, 11 October 08

A 5:00 a.m. wake-up call, breakfast required if we were to claim our train to Mongolia, one of the grandest rail journeys of the world. The mountain ridges render the Great Wall seemingly superfluous. Barren mountains yield to high-yielding plains, but the harvesting methods employed won't enrich anybody soon. American corn dominates, and any vehicle is pressed into the job of bringing in the crop. Diminutive tri-wheeled trucks, dwarfed by their loads, bicycles follow, nearly disappearing under heaps of stalks, before dairy cattle are drafted into service. The industriousness exhibited in these pre-industrial methods impress this ex-farm boy. This un-American agriculture appears at least to feed the masses.

12 October 08

My God, if ever, dear reader, you fancy feasting eyes upon absolutely nothing, go to the Gobi. Not even cacti mar the landscape, as far as an eye spies. We are dragged into this hellish desolation by a coal burner, as no one can live here to complain, except for us passengers who cough on that acrid smoke even when cocooned in our compartments. Possibly, my complaint comes only from the coal-fired samovars in every carriage.

To face this trial, you must first survive the border crossing. Be happy to see this soulless desert. The faces of Mongolian officials do not reassure western passengers who must surrender passports for three or four hours (if lucky), while officials, train staff, and rail workers exchange travelers and differently gauged tracks. Literally left hanging, until your car can be newly bogeyed, you do eventually move through darkness until dawnlight reveals…nothing. We endured hours of waiting for this? Make sure you plan toilet breaks carefully, as train toilets can be locked throughout the wait.

At some point you may choose to step off the train. Just be sure to be aboard when you need to be, ready to stand at attention beside your open baggage, all papers in hand, present and correct.

After rolling through nowhere for hours, the train halts in the smallest hamlet I've ever seen. Only one amenity stands clearly evident: a basketball hoop with an L.A. Lakers' backstop.

From there onward, slight signs of greenery signal the approach of animals. Horses appear first, promising Mongolian fantasies, followed by Bactrian camels, cattle, coyotes, sheep, goats, ground rodents and birds, then finally yaks. Mostly small horses occupy the mostly brown over-grazed environment. Horses in Ireland don't know how good they've got it.

When a town called Choir stops the train, enterprising urchins sell semi-precious stones outside the carriage doors. As their efforts were entirely precious, I purchased a few rocks. Unfamiliar with the currency, I made a better deal than expected. I swear to be more generous if ever I return. At least I didn't "sing to the Choir." Our Mongol guide nearly sings to be at home though. To each his own.

---

13 October 08

Yes, I did…eat horsemeat at B.D.'s Mongolian BBQ in U.B. (Ulaan Baatar), capital of Mongolia. B.D.'s is a western chain-franchise returning to its roots. I almost bought the t-shirt.

A poverty-stricken, drought-stricken country, shaded only by dominant neighbors, Mongolia reminds me of Mexico, only more so. Loads of Gringos hang out here too as no visa is required. Yanks working in China slip over to renew the visa. Sturdy street beggars also present a problem in U.B. The currency, once outside the state, holds only curiosity value. Tent cities, or ger districts, constitute slums here. These round, felt tents could be called yhurts or hogans. Navajo Indians would hold a strikingly similar lifestyle and appearance to traditional Mongols. Values must not be dissimilar.

Values tie Mongols even closer to Tibetans, who share their Lama Buddhism. To visit a temple where religion is still taken seriously comforted me, while simultaneously unsettling my soul. In Chinese temples my sole concern was for the soul of China.

Though Buddhists suffered horribly under Communism, Russian or Chinese, the Chinese in Inner Mongolia persecuted more thoroughly. Outer Mongolia, once the poor relation of Tibetan Buddhism, has its reviving temples envied now.

I underwent a spiritual revival of my own in dusty U.B., an unlikely location for one. Looking up at a blue sky, I spied a sliver of silver leaving streams of white vapor over azure. Déjà vu smacked me between the eyes. An identical vision sprang from childhood memory, from when I, at seven years of age, stood barefoot in a farmyard in upstate New York, day-dreaming about jet-flight to distant places. Never did I imagine on that farm, that I would ever stand in Outer Mongolia, spotting planes flying homewards. This moment may stand as the best of this trip, though I only gazed skyward at nothing not seen before.

As much as I'm enjoying myself, I hesitate to recommend this trip, as the weather has been exceptionally fine for the Aussies and me (my stormy insides aside). Weather can make or break a journey like this. Deciding to travel this late in the season did give me pause. I think I can recommend it, but suggest traveling in the opposite direction. Start in St. Petersburg, finish in Hong Kong. That choice evaded me this time. I'm fairly sure all border crossings would also go smoother west-to-east.

=== + ===

14 October 08

Having escaped from U.B.'s constraints, I stay today in a ger camp located in a national park protecting scenic mountains and high steppe. Though traditional nomadic life has largely disappeared, a little stays preserved here, even by our touristy camp. Time for time travel. The dramatic landscape calls out for horses, Genghis Khan and conquest. We're informed the Mongolian language holds no word for "whoa" or "please." That, and Mongolia's sweeping terrain, explains why the Mongol Empire (largest ever) managed to reach Germany, Turkey, Tibet, and the shores of Japan.

Pity, less than a quarter of the population even pretend to honor the old ways. Maybe a quarter million in this large, empty country still live as nomads. Many of the urban poor remain in yhurts though, burning wood and coal in small stoves, adding greatly to the serious pollution problem. However, even the nomads' yhurts are likely to have solar electricity, freezers, DVD players, satellite TV, and cellular phones.

Though horses are yet employed in herding, nomads prefer to own motor vehicles for making moves, and at least a motorbike for trips to town. They can't eat motorbikes though. Today all our group rode horses (the small native breed), a first for me. I thought I did well, with the jughead loaned to me, especially after being granted a gad. Since some had their mounts led for them, my natural ability drew comment, even from the Mongol horseman. My singing in the saddle impressed him as Mongols do that constantly. As a race, Mongols do not seem artsy or emotive, except when they're around horses.

Hiking and climbing in the national park is to-die-for, but I haven't killed myself yet—just close. Turtle Rock deserves special mention for its womb of stone, offering rebirth to hardy pilgrims. Beyond the Turtle, a cul-de-sac of cliffs holds high a holy shrine, my favorite so far. Its singular setting and unique artwork make it stand out. The paintings prove medieval Christians were not alone in their demonic visions of Hell. No place more fit for meditation than where the handiwork and devotion of both God and man are so evident and uplifting. We were fortunate to see this shrine, as during summer, monks only allow the faithful here.

15 October 08, 7:30 a.m.

On mornings like this, when standing where steep mountain sweeps down into rolling steppe, you have to say aloud to God, "Good job." Show a little appreciation and gratitude, or your soul will die. Though frost sparkles underfoot, sunbeams glint off snowy peaks. Out of the shadows, dry air does not chill. "Now," you might chide the Creator, "You're just showing off."

As an added bonus, the dryness preserves ancient artifacts, as the national museum in U.B. proves. Unexpectedly interesting, the dry facts are brought to life, and even more so by the cultural performance nearby: the Tumenekh Ensemble. I would probably have bypassed this show as too touristy and expensive, had I traveled alone. I would have been the poorer for not paying. Mongolian throat singing impresses uniquely.

Warning: life at ger camps can grow rougher than planned, as plumbing will freeze on October nights. Try Mongolian "knucklebone," a game of conquest, while you wait for thawing.

Travel may also be tricky departing Mongolia. Warned to accept no gifts or help from strangers, we never dreamed that would include the train staff. They provided superior slippers for our use. Disposable slippers are generally distributed on overnight trains in the East. Traditional felt foot-gear would not have been discarded though. Like ingénues, our tour of experienced travelers had been enlisted in a smuggling operation. Fortunately, we were warned in time to avoid a heavy fine, even imprisonment, at the Russian border. You may think that extreme for felt slippers, but you don't know what might have been slipped into the slippers. Moreover, customs inspection can operate as a scam too. The slippers could have provided an excuse for supplementing official wages. "Misunderstandings" escalate quickly with officialdom when you fail to understand local languages or customs.

Again, I advise: travel with a regular tour group to make being victimized by officials less likely. Presumably, the greasing of wheels is included in the price of the tour. You won't just disappear at least.

=== + ===

16 October 08

The 10- to 12-hour wait at the border affords a taste of incarceration. The train arrives too early for Mongolian officials, and Russian ones just like to make you wait, while they peruse your papers, possibly canceling your visa for no reason, reducing to dust your expensive plans and dreams. As all the while train toilets are locked, retain some Mongolian cash (and patience) for the station toilets.

Important: remember most of your Mongolian currency must be exchanged before departing U.B.

Any good news? Well, the stray mongrels hungrily circling our carriages show remarkably good manners and demeanor. I didn't expect that. More unexpectedly, the little duty-free sells Irish whiskey. That's two signs of a civilized country, but the train used to cross the border is the least civilized in the package. We're stuck on a local bucket, without even a dining-car, for two nights. Stock up in U.B.! The toilets fortunately kill my appetite for now.

═══ ✝ ═══

The long introduction to Siberian Russia could be called appropriate at least. Just looks like Montana to me though, until Goose Lake is reached. The change from Mongolia is decidedly dramatic. I cannot regret leaving such barrenness behind. Nice to see trees again. If I do shed a tear, it's for the Irish whiskey abandoned at my hotel in the rush to depart last night.

When I ran into a fellow mick at the theatre, I promised him a shot of Jameson's. If I had tried harder to keep that promise to a compatriot, I'd have caught my mistake in time. I trust he found both Irish pubs in U.B., plus the B.D. BBQ where we went again (for the horsemeat and the t-shirt).

The generally underdeveloped nature of the country made the touches of civilization more appreciated, none more so than our cultured and captivating guides. The tradition-bound freedom of the ger camp and the cultural show helped to explain how this severely limited society could produce such remarkable young women. How fortunate for me, that I am no longer young.

═══ ✝ ═══

17 October 08

I was also glad to reach Russia because I had greatly feared not leaving China alive. Dysentery descended into diabolical depths. At the Great Wall, I nearly crapped myself just worrying about crapping myself. One hope carried me across the border: if I could just cross the border before hospitalization, all visas honored, I might finish my circuit sometime, if I didn't die.

In Mongolia I recovered only enough to suffer a relapse in Russia. This time, I suspect the restaurant staff of deliberate poisoning, due to an earlier incident. The greatest drawback to traveling with a package tour, however intimate, is the loss of dietary control. Dining socially on prepaid meals, maybe pre-prepared meals, I had little choice but to dig in happily, pretending to appreciate local fare, and worrying later. Usually that beats dining alone anyway.

In spite of the above experience, I did enjoy Irkutsk, a university town, reminiscent of Poland's Cracow, full of young people and history. Our own local guide is a most striking and accomplished student of history. Sundowners Tours selects clever guides carefully. The local museum would probably be interesting anyway, even without the blond and brainy Olga, of the mysterious eyes. The building, purpose-built, presents in itself a treasure.

Irkutsk, scenically situated on the Angara River, truly embraces the sole outflow of Lake Baikal.

18 October 08

En route to the lake, we visit on the river's bank a wooden village museum. Interestingly, what spurs most interest in this museum is how little village life has altered over centuries. From what we could spy, life remains pretty primitive and wood based. This particular collection of log structures was designated a museum when moved here before a hydroelectric dam created new banks for the river. The People's Party had previously evicted the rural proletariat to electrify the city of Irkutsk.

The highway through this sparsely populated area Khrushchev only built to show off Lake Baikal to Eisenhower on a trip that never happened, due to the famous U2 incident. His loss is our gain.

Had the U.S. president visited, I might have heard more before about this place which deserves its place among the natural wonders of the world. By far the Earth's largest body of fresh water, 80 percent of its bountiful flora and fauna are endemic to this isolated lake. Its own breed of seals surprised me most.

In a mile-deep lake, these creatures are able to dive deep enough to eat a fish which would merely melt on the surface. Pressure holds together the bubbles of fish oil on which these seals fatten. The seals should thrive with no natural enemy but man, as remarkably few of the latter live around here. Even fewer protect the natural wonders of this region from exploitation however. The world has been lucky so far. I feel privileged to have viewed this jewel in its pristine setting. A splendid mountain-banked sea, this shining masterpiece of God, nearly overwhelms its viewer, on yet another bright-eyed day.

The great outdoors enlivens my soul even as my own insides kill my body. Two outside factors may contribute to this crime. One warning I owe anyone who travels due to this book. All over Asia, used toilet paper does not hygienically disappear down sewer pipes. Rather, a small wastebasket (often the only one in a hotel room or train) collects this refuse. Local t.p. proves too tough, we're told, for local septic systems. I tend towards bringing my own tissues to flush regardless.

The second poor practice common in Asia is a failure to double-sheet beds, even in five-star hotels. Heavy duvets employed instead render sleepers alternately too warm or too cold. Overheating rooms on this seasonal cusp happens often. If a window to cooler, more polluted, air can be opened, the traveler with whom you share may not be open to that idea.

From the finest hotel in Irkutsk, we moved to pleasant chalets with veranda views of Lake Baikal. Nearby, the museum of endemic marine biology provides more intimate views of Baikal life. Avail of the sauna at the chalets for intimate views I won't detail here, but beware of the birch switches.

---

19 October 08

After one night, we returned to town for further touring, and an exceptional meal at a very fancy restaurant. Distracted by my stomach, I forgot the stick from a mile deep in the Grand Canyon. Ah, well, I'd already broken it, back on a Mongol mountain. Next time down, I'll go for the t-shirt.

As from dinner we went straight to the station, returning for a stick would not have been wise. I would like to revisit that restaurant someday though, for the menu and ambience, if not for my stick. While its Russian name remains unremembered, I could locate it again, in one of the few well-maintained traditional wooden buildings in this city of fire hazards.

In the countryside, traditional Siberian architecture prevails even more. Along the train tracks, similar tracts of squat log cabins intermittently emerge from vast forest. Vegetable gardens attached to each cottage might feed anywhere from one to eight occupants. In each settlement, about two dozen wee wooden cottages nestle along dirt alleys without mothering from any large ecclesiastic or civic building.

As the Transiberian Express speeds into the setting sun, we riders can see Old Mother Russia remains alive, if not exactly well.

Monday, 20 October 08

All of today saw more of the same scenery. Villages of cottages with patches of veggies break periodically the monotony of birch-brushed evergreen. Now and then, a large field or small city will show itself briefly. If we stop, all disembark regardless, though little beyond station platforms can be observed. Every opportunity to stretch our legs is appreciated, or to stretch our stomachs with the purchase of traditional fare from Babushkas, or of junk food from kiosks.

Though the food might be dodgy, the greater threat to your digestion is the danger of the train's departure without you. Car attendants locking toilets for 15 minutes before stations until 15 minutes after them, also adds to the nervousness of travelers. Any delay might mean an hour without a loo, while you consume unfamiliar fodder of doubtful origin. If you do find a crude cubicle, you might lose a train.

Fully digesting any travel announcements fed to us, continues unlikely.

Despite having viewed the movie, "Transiberian," I allow an overly-friendly, English-speaking tourist to latch on to me, drawing the attention of a Russian policeman, allegedly anxious to practice his English while on holiday. Both seem fine fellows, but the alcohol flows, as does inappropriate enquiry.

Preferring to think the best of my traveling companions, I'm still glad to stay sober. Slainte to Dominic and Vladimir. As an American, I might owe a compatriot a look out, and ought to return any courtesy offered by a native foreigner. However, I do admit my nervousness as a cast of characters continues to build for a re-enactment of the above film. I don't want to audition for the role of victim.

Once, when traveling in Italy, I rejoiced to review Sienna's famous Palio celebration, re-enacted for film cameras. I'm less thrilled to take part in a real-life re-enactment of a film thriller.

=== + ===

Tuesday, 21 October 08

Two nights on one train constitutes the longest session of rail travel in this rail package. I delight to note our band rates this service highest so far, with the best bedding and cleanest toilets. Lighting and heating have not worked perfectly, but performed ideally for me. A dining car we'll mark "present."

A passing commuter train makes me count my blessings. The workers only get wooden benches. God's mercy on those poor blighters. The Russian populace looks nearly as unhealthy as America's. Too much alcohol and empty carbs clog both diets.

=== + ===

Strangely, along our rural route, almost no grazing animal can be seen, nor fenced pasture. No barnyard fowl, indeed, no farm life of any sort has been noticed for hundreds of miles. Occasionally, sad little cemeteries reveal covered crosses in a distant grove. Is this dearth of life, or of variety, a legacy of collectivization? Or, is the cause more current? Our guides are not always happy to answer questions.

- * -

CHAPTER 3

Europe

5:00 p.m., Ekaterinburg

On the boundary fence of Europe and Asia a city of 1.5 million comfortably sits. Only an outpost in the time of Peter the Great (late 17th century), Ekaterinburg had big ideas even then. Unfortunately, the greatest historical claim for this city named for a czarina is the murder of a czarina, along with her entire family, including Nicholas II. In 2000 AD, a monumental church has been constructed on the spot, nearly canonizing these holy martyrs of the people and Christianity. Really?!

--- + ---

Park Inn Hotel

We declare this city civilized, due to my hotel bar offering not only Jameson's, but Tullamore Dew. On the downside, directly before those bottles of Irish in the lobby bar, a fat cigar smoker (both cigar and smoker) looks exactly like a Bond movie villain, complete with two long-legged, black-booted blonds. Irish pubs no longer allow smoking. Here even the dining room provides ashtrays on every table. The villain fails to spoil our superlative meal however. The staff proved impeccable.

--- + ---

22 October 08

Breakfast satisfied the most since Hong Kong.

The aforementioned Shrine to the Royal Martyrs we toured today. The crypt, exactly where the Bolsheviks executed the Romanoffs, the Orthodox Church keeps as "The Chapel of the Blood." More moving, the monument outside the church depicts the royal family's descent down 23 steps to their destruction.

An old soviet monument, facing the new shrine, had been deliberately, symbolically, built with its back to the original church on the square. Ha! Yet another chapel chimes in its defiance of Marxist doctrine here. Dedicated to St. Elizabeth, "the German Princess," this small edifice honors the Czar's sister-in-law, executed elsewhere, whose body now rests—miraculously preserved—in Jerusalem.

The very talented sculptor, Greenburg, who created the royal homage, also produced the emotive memorial that commemorates nearby the Soviet Army defeated in Afghanistan.

You can walk to another museum of particular interest in this region, the Mineral Museum.

From the Shrine of the Royal Martyrs, the tour took us to the Monastery of the same, deep in the endless forest, where the Bolshies burned and buried the Romanoff remains. This monastic settlement was carefully constructed traditionally, all of wood, without nails. Seven separate chapels represent the seven victims, also represented by many sacred relics and icons. Tolling bells and chanting monks complete the effect.

From the memorial monastery we journeyed on to another place of division, but not of sorrow. Our crossing from Asia into Europe we celebrated with champagne, chocolate and certificates. One more milestone I have passed before the last.

=== + ===

23 October 08

Moscow and tomorrow, here we come. Ekaterinberg Station

deserves a look-in even if you're not leaving. Once you've left, the interesting views (and the locomotive) pull you into Europe. Scenery and social organization alters decidedly. Czarist and/or communist policy must have directed the odd development of Russian Asia. Aside from all water flowing westward away from Asia (to a magical lake), the land in Europe is, by nature and development, immediately more varied and colorful.

Village streets continue only mud though. Clay cakes the cars coming into city streets. Very little paint do Russians expend on any wooden structure in town or country. As for concrete, Stalin stands condemned a butcher as an architect too. None of the newer buildings match the flair displayed in Beijing.

The tour's most disappointing aspect, here and in Siberia (Mongolia and China too), undoubtedly is the quantity of trash strewn along the tracks. Aggravation.

═══ ✛ ═══

9:00 a.m., 24 October 08

Ah, Moscow in the morning! Nadia guides our wee band here, wowing us all with the breadth of her knowledge. Yes, she's fairly fair as well. Thanx again, Sundowners. The warmth of Moscow in late October surprises. Eleven million citizens with 860 years of history, this capital, political and ecclesiastical, also surprises by being the first grand, historic western metropolis of this trip. A city of churches, "Christ the Savior" rules, as the premier cathedral of all Russian Orthodoxy, though last built—or rebuilt.

Originally opened in 1883, after 45 years of construction, the massive edifice was leveled by the Commies, and replaced by something more prosaic. In the year 2000, an exact replica replaced the replacement in four and a half years. The new power of the old religion astonishes me. Such success I do suspect.

On opposite sides of the church, two metal statues stand

clearly visible, but concealing ironies I will reveal. A memorial to Alexander II praises "the Emancipator," the czar who freed the serfs. The revolutionaries of "The People's Will," enemies of reform, who murdered the czar, were hung by Alexander III—including the elder brother of Lenin (who would execute the latter Alexander's son).

A monumental sculpture honoring Peter the Great, founder of the Russian Navy, towers above the Muscovy River. This heroically posed, imaginative memorial, a famous Italian artist created, reportedly to represent Christopher Columbus. Failing to unload it in America, the sculptor sold it to Russia, as Peter. Even were this rumor false, siting the work in Moscow remains controversial. So far inland, Moscow was replaced as capital by Peter, with St. Petersburg, gateway harbor to the West, created by his own great self.

More impressive than all the above, consider New Maiden's Convent for aristocratic women, Peter's sister included. He confined her for plotting against him. Call that a vocational hazard. Built in the same fortress style as the Kremlin, the convent holds better corpses than the czars. Within and adjacent to the walls, Mother Russia has interred her most legendary children, heroes of the arts and sciences, as well as the military and politics.

The Kremlin itself, on Red Square with St. Basil's Cathedral, Lenin's Tomb, and G.U.M. (the old state department store), anciently fortifies a capitol complex, of both czars and commies. G.U.M. looks like a prosperous, multi-level mall now, with an admirable cafeteria. Lenin's tomb we bypassed, so not to lose our appetites. It lacked the religious hysteria of Mao's mausoleum anyway. St. Basil's has it though. Typical of old Orthodox churches, the cathedral actually jumbles a collection of little chapels, ten in fact. St. Basil's is merely the last and least in what is properly called "the Cathedral for the Intercession of Blessed Mary." The cathedral commemorated Ivan the Terrible's success against the Mongol yoke.

Not far from the New Maiden, Maidenfield was named for the tribute in maidens paid the Mongol horde prior to Ivan's success. Not nuns. Sundowner supplied a Mongol maiden as our regular guide.

Victory Park celebrates another success over barbarians: the defeat of German Huns in the Great Patriotic War (WWII). Opened for the 50th anniversary of victory, the park and its monuments appear suitably massive, and include a museum (we never visited).

Across the city from the Kremlin ridge, Stalin topped another bluff with the State University of Moscow, largest and most prestigious in the country. As the pinnacle of the scholastic summit, the largest of Stalin's "seven sisters" rules the landscape. Not big fat ladies, these less than edifying edifices circle the city center, more oppressively than impressively.

--- + ---

After a long sprint of sight-seeing, following a longer rail ramble, any hotel might look good, but I am convinced of the singularity of my Moscovite abode. *The Sovietsky*, another grand old dam of Stalin (not the one who shot herself), less domineering than the seven sisters, curtsies gracefully (for an old lady) towards shabby chic. Her wide hallways and showcase staircase, walked by legendary legs, present a permanent movie set, in which I enjoy playing, though I probably would not enjoy the movie. That film, with this set, and this cast, would turn towards surreal, with little dialogue, all of it sub-titled.

--- + ---

25 October 08

The Sovietsky serves the best breakfast of this tour. Anytime I voluntarily eat seconds of asparagus, you know it's good. The medley of flavors did not require the medley of music from the grand piano, but the medleys complimented nicely. Delicious.

By way of contrast, we return to the Kremlin, a forbidding fortress, one of the largest in Europe, containing more churches and palaces than you could shake a stick at—if you dared. The highlight for me, St. Michael's Church, embraces the burial places of every czar before Peter the Great. Aside from displaying the most color to my eye (physically and figuratively), this church provided acapella singers for my ears. Old Russian hymns performed by five voices, singing unfathomed words, can make the eyes weep of anyone who has ears.

Though within the Kremlin walls, the Armory requires a separate ticket but is well worth the price. You'll find the most stunning royal collection ever seen anywhere. I'm certain. Everything, from Faberge eggs to inlaid suits of amour, waits for your appreciation.

Escalators in and out of Moscow's Metro could make your nose bleed. I'm able to pen this note while riding one. Other than the moving mountain, I am less than impressed with the rest so far. If I wasn't an experienced subway rider, I'd be lost now. Instead, I have, unassisted, attained a selected destination, and returned prior to an appointed time. "No. 57," the cafeteria in the G.U.M. store, was the appointed place, at dinner time. Punctuality was demanded prior to a charming cultural evening at the Old English Merchants' House. There, vaunted vaulted chambers have provided great acoustics since the reigns of Good Queen Bess and Ivan the Terrible. For me though, the genuine sacred music, accidentally discovered at Orthodox vigil services today, sounded more...um, let's just leave it at "more."

---

26 October 08

Turning back the clock gained me an hour, a gift from God—sinful to scorn. I did go back to bed, and did need it badly. But after, I got busy.

On the Metro: Komsomolskaya, Revolution Square, and Arbotskaya Stations do indeed earn the 19 ruble ($1.00) entry-fee to the People's Underground Palaces. Come out at Arbotskaya Street for window shopping and people watching. About one in 20 women in Moscow atavistically descend from a race of long-limbed Viking Valkyries. With boots on, they scare me—with bells on.

Traveling in a time of global financial crisis puts an edge on the dull commonplace. While currencies climb and collapse, foreclosures skyrocket, and banks fail, common folk continue to pay $12 for a cuppa and cake at Starbucks, both in Beijing and Moscow.

The Sportiva Station delivers the medieval New Maidens' Convent, and the cemetery attached. Most of the most famous names in Russian history live on here. Predictably, but annoyingly anyway, the monuments list all names cyrillicly, and no guides (in paper or person) are visibly available. Nevertheless, the memorials appear impressive and expressive. I did definitely identify Yeltsin's and Khrushchev's markers. I considered removing my shoe to bang on the latter stone, but could not convince myself that everyone would appreciate my American humor.

In the opposite direction from the same station, you can find the largest "market" in Moscow. Acres of stalls, in various stages of permanence, offer every form of apparel, plus other items of interest for bargain hunters. Be warned though, foreign bargain hunters will be disappointed, as Russia imports most consumer goods, like the U.S., at prices I would not ordinarily "write home about."

Our tour had nearly departed Moscow before the inevitable meltdown struck. Unexpectedly, I, the obviously anti-social outsider, did not trigger the China syndrome. Indeed, if anything, I soothed hurt feelings, and applied first-aid to damaged egos. After assisting in the general venting and cooling process, I am confident our group can hold together for one more stop, but we won't be all better, not ever. Why all the steam? Depends on who you ask. Maybe the reaction came from something as small as an atom. For me to say more would cause trouble though. I remain loyal to the group, my travel companions.

--- + ---

27 October 08, St. Petersburg

At last. Five million plus in people, this burg offers 700 churches and countless palaces, perfectly arranged. St. Nicholas', or "the Wedding Cake," delights me most. You'll find it on Seven Bridges Square (with the eight bridges). The piece de resistance in mansions must be the czar's Winter Palace, of which the Hermitage Art Museum forms merely a part. Inside the Hermitage, a jewel box of a theatre (once the private performance space for Catherine the Great), provides today's highlight, even before an intimate rendition of Swan Lake. In fact, the happy ending tacked on to that tragedy nearly spoiled my day. Geesh.

Did Tchaikovsky live happily ever after too? No.

Never mind, I enjoyed the oboe music anyway. That instrument never fails to hit a melancholic note, no matter what melody is dictated. Such a plaintive voice.

--- + ---

28 October 08

Three million works of art reside in the Hermitage. DaVinci, Rembrandt, Picasso, everybody who was ever anybody (after they were dead) is represented here, and by works seldom seen in the West. Despite an acid attack on a Rembrandt, the museum leaves its collection open to the closest inspection. Dimwits with flashbulbs attack the paintings constantly, while attendants stand idly by. I decided to make a couple happy snappers a little less happy myself. The war, between painting and photography in the art world, should not be taken to this level. I'm ready to start dropping cameras into buckets of paint, okay?

The Spanish Room earned most respect from me, but my most preferred painting isn't hung there. Possibly its placement at the end of a hallway drew me to Troyan's *"Departing for Market."* Maybe my being a farm boy and a pilgrim made a difference, but objectively, great skill in the artist is revealed in this masterpiece. Without words, and from beyond the grave, the painter spoke to me. That's art.

You'll see for yourself, of course, but many different works will be hung by then.

For lunch we tried "the Idiot," named after the Dostoevsky tome, not the chef.

Of churches, I'd say St. Isaac's "museum" almost earns the entry fee.

--- + ---

29 October 08

The czar's summer palace, outside St. Petersburg, nearly as palatial as the townhouse, looks best from the angle of the past. Peering from 1945, you appreciate that the entire property required complete restoration after German troops lifted the siege of Leningrad, leaving behind only incendiary devices. Though some treasures had been removed beforehand and returned, most of the interiors needed replacing to present the present vision of gold and silk, marble and mirror, mahogany and ebony, crystal and amber.

The amber room takes the prize for Art and Artifice in Restoration.

Called the largest piece of jewelry in the world, an entire room paneled in patterned amber, no way would the Nazis leave behind. Ironically, gifted to Peter the Great by Prussia's Frederick I, the present was only reclaimed by Hitler's Prussians, and returned by a German Corp. who paid for the current reproduction. The fullness of irony you cannot perceive until history informs that the palace grounds began as an Indian gift by Peter to his one-time best pal.

One should mention here, that all commerce and civilization in the Baltic region was once based on the amber trade. That trade flourishes still, though much of what's marketed now is manufactured.

As important as the fanciful baroque and classical architecture and décor, St. Petersburg palaces receive coats of pastel paints, which speak to a populace burdened under notoriously heavy skies.

Sky blue with bright white, sunny yellow trimmed by moonlight, pink and pearly, all combine with uniform geometric lines, in buildings and gardens, to create a totally pleasing effect. One street, 220 yards long by 22 yards wide, stretches between colonnades (22 yards high) from a Venetian canal bridge to an artfully placed theatre. That theatre is only one of many in this city of culture.

I don't believe I've ever met a metropolis more easy on the eye. History teaches, however, that "easy" ain't the word to describe this effect. First, all palaces, parks and boulevards only imitate originals in Paris, Florence and Venice. Nothing just happened, or grew organically in St. Petersburg. All appeared by design, carefully constructed on the backs of serfs, and even unwilling noblemen.

"Copies of imitation" more closely describes the city's look, as most of it must have been smashed in the siege of Leningrad (WWII—St. Petersburg). For 900 days the city suffered one of history's longest, most destructive sieges.

The Nazis war machine, not known for respecting person and property, had never failed to take or destroy anything—until Leningrad. Hence, Hitler confidently had printed invitations for a champagne celebration in the city's Astoria Hotel. He had to cancel. Party poopers.

This Venice of the North continues to be spared from barbarians. Besides planning regulations, the soft silt of this delta prevents the erection of modern monstrosities to mar the four-story horizon, ruled by church steeples.

Surprisingly, another height problem also finds relief here. No army of blond amazons stalks the streets as they do in Moscow. Explain that. Maybe the petite, fine-featured women around here represent a legacy of the siege's starvation? No? Some insane Stalinist purge?

--- + ---

Three hours suffices to stroll the whole city center. That allows for checking entry times and fees, and for checking out the wee weemin, plus for checking the map after getting lost. Starting at a civilized time, you could still be done by lunch. I recommend the Armenian restaurant named after Khrushchev, at the far end of Razezzhaya Ulitsa. After coffee, return to whatever attractions you have selected in the a.m. (Better not be the women.)

Another warning: if you've picked the Winter Palace, you're done picking for the day.

Third warning: Peter the Great's vision has not escaped modernity entirely. Chaos caused by cars had better be bested before it worsens.

Finally: nature still rules the night. Every night from 1:00 a.m. until 5:00 a.m., every bridge is raised for river traffic. Cars can go jump then. Everyone in town must swap stories of pickles that raised bridges have put them in. I bet many lies have been born, or done to death, by drawbridges.

--- + ---

30 October 08

I had a hard time escaping St. P. myself, and that's no lie. First, not-so-beautiful Belarus decides everyone on the train for Poland must apply for (and pay for) a visa before traversing their territory. Whatever the cost in cash, I couldn't afford the three days needed. As the Baltic States make no such demand, I took that roundabout route instead, but *not* as you'd expect: via Baltic Station.

Fortunately, Vitibsk Station sits closer, as I needed to drag my bags there in the rain, unfortunately. Tickets I'd wisely purchased previously. Sans assistance, I needed plenty of time for that. Now that the tour is over, I'm on my own again. Unable to speak Russian, I was able to buy a ticket in a station full of ticket-kiosks for other trains. I needed to find the kiosk for a ticket to Poland—but not for the Polish train.

On arriving for departure, I noted my ticket's date, 30 October 2007, a year out-of-date! Rejoining the ticket queue, I learned 2007 meant 8:07 p.m. Duh. Car and seat number still needed identifying anyway.

Once entrained, I considered conditions grimmer than a Greyhound bus; and when attendants admitted a real hound, I tried to bribe my way forward—futilely. Yet, the night did pass regardless, and could easily have proved harder on me. The dog behaved better than some other passengers.

Halloween 31 October 08

Latvian and Lithuanian countryside could pass for any of the countryside recently passed. Possibly the small plots appear more prosperous. Nearing Poland, however, the large fields of mechanized agriculture take over, and remind me of the plains of Castile. Cattle, however, are only tethered in pairs here—here and there. Roads remain unpaved. Also divergent from Russia (and similar to Spain), Roman Catholic churches suddenly rise to herald the Latin alphabet's use, and the absence of Russian Orthodox authoritarianism. Thank God. You thought Catholicism was bad?

In the first Catholic church I have been able to enter since California, I lit a candle for my mother's recovery. A "penal rosary" of Baltic amber I bought from a vendor at Vilna's Gate of the Chapel. "Our Lady of the Dawn" displays for veneration its miraculous icon, a national symbol of Lithuania. My mum will especially appreciate this, as she raised us to pray the rosary daily, with a special intention of freedom for the captive Baltic nations, along with the destruction of the Iron Curtain and Berlin Wall. Only total destruction of Godless communism would in fact satisfy Mother, and cease her harassment of Himself.

Never underestimate the power of prayer. I'm not making any claims personally. I stick to the facts: we prayed; the evil empire was overturned. Honestly, though I prayed till my knees went knobby, I am amazed at what has come to pass in my lifetime.

By the by, religion is taken seriously here. All Souls' Day attracts none of the sacrilegious nonsense perpetuated in America.

1 November 08

Vilna now bustles prosperously, but Old Vilna paused to welcome me, with much charm and some poignancy. Intending only to pass a couple hours until the next train, I lingered too long and stayed overnight. A hard run helped me to salvage my ticket at least. I don't mind being stuck here now. Proud Vilna looks very attractive, but deep suffering has etched lines into her face.

I suffered some in Vilna myself. Firstly someone sent me on a wild goose chase. Would a tourist info person do that deliberately? Help locating a tourist hostel is all I sought. A toilet was needed more than a bed. Only a sadist would purposely send me so far out of my way.

When the hostel was located, quite near the station, it had free internet at least, presenting my first opportunity to make travel plans confidently. Having no luck with cut-rate airlines, I turned to a travel service advertising discounted Aer Lingus tickets to Ireland. Scam possibilities considered, I carefully gave credit details in return for a ticketing pledge. Fine. Yet, checking for confirmation, I faced more demands for personal details.

I would gladly drop the whole thing, but the details already supplied suffice for them to debit my account legally, citing my failure to comply as justification. Indeed, a huge cancellation fee may lurk in the fine print. Before I could obtain any help, I had to catch the train to Warsaw. Time did not even permit me to spend remaining Lithuanian currency. Quite willing for sharpies to take advantage at the border, I could not find a smidgen of overpriced food, toiletries or souvenirs. Fools.

I wasn't foolish enough to miss the Polish train by wandering too far. Now I ride in comparative comfort, except for my grumbling stomach.

Arriving blindly in Warsaw after dark, I managed to locate the ideal hostel (Nathan's Villa) near the station—but not too near.

You know what I mean. I could not enjoy my stay, however, occupied with trying to sort out my plane ticket problem. Granted only 24 hours to comply with the unreasonable demands, I phoned my card provider for help. This emergency call, allegedly free from anywhere in the world, costs plenty from Poland.

Long struggles to disentangle myself meant going to bed hungry, but not until after a midnight trip to the U.S. embassy nearby. I do hope Uncle Sam never bills me for the call made there, an expensive worthless call to my credit provider. A lot of soft jazz music, they followed with soft soap. The upshot: the credit company can do nothing, and I can continue hoping for the best. Just great.

---

2 November 08, Sunday

I confess you find me in the McDonald's under Warsaw's Central Station. I am embarrassed; however, McD's does seem the appropriate place to celebrate having traveled around the Earth on earth. My first night in Asia I celebrated the same. When something has claws already sunk into my intestines, I don't fancy experimenting with the local tucker. True, I did say I would die happy if I could just reach this spot, but if this is dying, I don't feel too delighted.

Continuing to cross the continent by rail has been considered and re-considered, but Europe and America I have already crossed, and criss-crossed again. As if to confirm a decision to abandon trains, the strap of my large duffle bag snapped today. Metal fatigue. If it's tired, imagine how I feel. Imagine what that heavy bag has been doing to my bones. If I ever go traveling again, purchasing a proper backpack will take precedence. Also pertinent, Eurail Passes do not extend to Poland.

Aboard the Cracow Express, my last train trip, I'm playing

chess. My greatest disappointment with the Transiberian was not playing more chess. Only one game was granted, probably by a Mongolian.

Getting ticketed today, and correctly seated on the right train—without knowing Polish—provided an excellent warm-up exercise for my brain. Finding a chess player? That was just luck. Incidentally, I have now circled the world without losing a match. That was just lucky too, though chess abhors chance.

※ ✦ ※

3 November 08

Wait till you hear, you won't believe what happened to me today. I woke in a Cracow hostel, not a crack house, to discover having been placed in a mixed dorm. My own body distracted me from the unexpected view. No, not that. My foot protruded from the bedclothes to reveal enormous nails, unclipped throughout the trip. Then I realized that my female roommates, probably annoyed by my snoring, had affixed false nails to that foot. Oh, very funny.

Well, I just continued to snore, not wanting to give them the satisfaction of a big reaction. Next, a male staff member (no pun) entered the room, and commented to the girls about my late snooze. Having an hour until check out, I was within my rights. Giggling with the girls, he suggested pouring a bottle of water on me.

Not really asleep, I grabbed the bottle to douse him. Not to be outdone in front of the women, the jackass ducked into the loo to dip water from the bowl. Stepping way over the line, he threw that at me. I only stormed out of the room to clean off.

Ah, but after, in the kitchen I pulled bags of ice from a freezer. Finding the offender in a meeting with co-workers, I shouted what he'd done, and clubbed him with the frozen water. The ice-man cometh, and beats the hell out of an ejit.

Now, just to prove that you can't believe everything you read, none of the above is true. In reality, I woke up at this point in the saga. Except for waking in a co-ed dorm, all turned out to be a dream. This nightmare suggests a deep unease at traveling alone again, sleeping in low-end hostels.

Having said that, I must add that I've never seen a city better served by hostels than Cracow is. Reserving ahead isn't really necessary, though the town is jumping (more than on my previous visit), even in this off season. I notice also that prices have hiked, across the board. The Polish currency, the zloty, does fine against the dollar, and joining the euro will undoubtedly bring inflation. However, the Poles seem to prosper. In fact, they're starting to put on weight. Woman particularly. Not good.

The western lifestyle and diet must be doing damage. Maybe a bigger culprit than fried carbs is the birth control pill. The full cost of the sexual revolution will never be counted. The winners are the losers, and they don't want to know.

I noted the pervasiveness of American pop music, over Polish folk music, during my previous trip. The dated tunes were not without charm though. Somewhat quaint, they yet were a radical expression of anti-communist sentiment. Two years on, Poles have caught up with current U.S. pop culture: gangster rap and sex videos, played in Micky D's. That is without charm. Oh when will we all be truly free?

Also sad to see, a huge mall has sprung up in the heart of town, with all the usual suspect chains. Beats them being outside town, beating the city center, I guess.

11:30 a.m., 4 November 08

A promise I've kept, to the people of Prague, and to you, my darlin' readers. I pledged to give Prague a second chance. Well, I arrived at 7:00 a.m., and am not impressed yet. I'm confirmed in my opinion (refer to *A Pilgrim's Progress—Possibly*) that a city this dependent on tourism should try harder.

Like last time, my train pulled into Prague, not at the Central Station, but at a peripheral one. Uncertain, where to jump off, my choice looked familiar, like the one desired. Later I learned the train never would reach Central Station, which stands in dreadful disrepair. The grandiose belle époque shell appears derelict, while underground an ant colony of scurrying humanity hides. Only a strong second effort found the tourist info booth that dispensed free maps. When I found the public loo, I also discovered a 10 krona charge ($0.60). McDonald's, here we come again.

At the station where I first arrived, no tourist info could be found, nor even a bureau de change. I did spy an ATM and a metro ticket machine. Proud to say, I worked out their operation. The foreigners in front of me paid too much.

=== + ===

Great, something that does impress: the strikingly sited, beaux arts National Museum. Though closed today by malchance, its grand portico I employed to eat my lunch, and to feast upon the view of St. Wenslaus' Square. In turn the royal saint stares from horseback down a broad boulevard to Old Prague. The way is painstakingly paved in stones of two square inches and reddish hue.

The merest mound beneath that pavement, directly before the museum, makes a mini but very moving monument. Jan Palach immolated himself on that spot in 1968. He may have been inspired by the equestrian monument before me. No pedestrian do-gooder this, a royal warrior rides here, a nation's patron saint. Under the majestic memorial, young activists have set up an artfully forceful display, a polemic about resistance to communist rule, encouraging a continuing fight for freedom.

=== + ===

I surrendered to capitalist imperialism by entering the McD's on St. Wenslaus' Square. Sorry, the toilets are always free, and nearly free of filth. At least a half dozen McDonald's grasp at the proletariat.

Escaping, I yielded next to the ornate historical and the ugly history that is Old Prague. How right of me to give this civic splendor another chance. Everywhere I cast an eye another tower or steeple peeks back at me, and speaks in whispers above the cobbled streets, busy squares and quiet courtyards, about the lives lived here where I lightly tread. The entire city center, both sides of the river, connected by a famously fanciful bridge, rightly thrives under UNESCO protection. Hell, I would defend this belle damsel myself, so don't dare say a word against her. Even if she behaves too bohemian or bourgeois for Catholic taste, don't say that.

My favorite notion pictures Mozart strolling these very lanes to these same theatres and churches. Don Giovanni premiered here. He would promenade arm-in-arm with a friend through the Clementine, the Jesuit University, towards a towered bridge, itself a work of art. Wouldn't he climb the hill to the castle too, where a royal palace and cathedral rule the view? Surely so.

I wager the cathedral was open when *he* presented himself. I arrived in time to witness the change of the palace guard at least, and to view the splendid collection of spires and flying buttresses the gothic cathedral displays, unchanged for centuries. From the doorway of an even older basilica next door, classical music sweetly sounds. Mozart maybe.

Certainly his ingenious symphonies fill other churches below. Prague performs more orchestral music than any city I've ever entered, and I have toured all of Europe. After all, most Bohemians are born to be musicians, and most musicians become bohemians.

=== † ===

All Aboard!

Vienna, even Paris, would die to present restaurants of such ambience as Prague's. Much free music can be enjoyed in this town if you're willing to stand outside like me. The same approach outside restaurants rewards far less—unless you're Scottish.

Stop me if you've heard this one. A Scotchie and his lassie were walking arm in arm through Glasgow, where they passed an eatery emitting a delicious aroma. "Ach, Jimmy," she says, "Did you smell that?" "Aye, I did. Would you like me to walk you past again?"

Someday, I'll return with more time and money. Now I need to return underground for a train to a train away from Prague's embrace.

=== + ===

Having praised Prague, I should also offer warning here. Something sinister and desperate snakes beneath the surface of this city. I don't mean the subway. Gangs of pick-pockets, other people-preyers or purveyors, famously pervade the disarmingly quaint urban spaces provided. Hence, I had reason to be nervous when approached underground by an overly-friendly attractive female.

While I felt for my wallet, she smiled and nodded, greeting me in English as if we'd already met. Not recognizing her pretty face from my one day in town, my eyes darted to spot her minders. Then, she said the magic word. "Camino." We had completed pilgrimage together in Spain. Though I still didn't remember her, my nervous grin widened to a delighted smile. When she asked what I was doing in Prague, and where I was going, a long story ran around the world quite quickly, bringing me to this platform for the train to the train to Cracow. Like an angel sent, she warned me about boarding the wrong train, and directed me to another tunnel, one which had earlier turned me away, with a wickedly misleading sign.

On the right train, another young woman, nearly as lovely,

insisted on giving up her seat, despite my protests. Finally, I accepted as graciously as possible—for her sake—though I am not as old and tired as I look.

Here's the oddest thing. Turns out I was boarding the correct subway initially, but would not have realized that until too late, unless I had gone the wrong way first. Understand, no one had bothered to mention that the train to Cracow does not depart from the same station where it arrives.

Now do you see what I mean about Prague?

Worse yet, due to other misdirection, I had forgotten to validate my subway ticket. Pulling into the station, I faced arrest and fines, besides missing my train and plane. Emerging unchecked however, I resolved to give my good ticket to any poor person sighted. Only after learning I had come to the wrong station, did I realize who was most in need.

Still, having wisely allowed an extra hour for complying with Murphy's Law, I could retrace my steps, and put all to right. Even aboard the train to Cracow, I had to move twice to find the right seat. Though all seats were unreserved, the right seat would be one continuing to my destination. You really can't be too careful about the destinations of each carriage, especially on night trains.

---

5 November 08

Back in Cracow, feeling grotty from two days on trains, I refused a Polish friend's kind offer of his flat, and immediately sought a hostel near the station. The Garden House I recommend. Aside from many fine free features, the hostel is located on Florianska St., famous for its medieval gate, and near the cathedral on the Duomo Plaza. Though also close to the station, trains don't run past the windows.

Today I dedicate just to showering, shaving, laundering, emailing, and collecting luggage.

--- + ---

6 November 08

Having left the hostel at the last moment train time allowed, after garnering a good breakfast and a flight-confirming email, I grabbed the final train for catching my plane, given the two-hours-prior rule. The herd of wild economy customers had already gathered for their migration with Ryanair. I checked in fairly fast regardless, before remembering two knives and two scissors still in my carry on. (On trains, no one cares.) Never mind, I pressed on, after quickly devising a trick for bringing knives through security.

No, I better not share that.

Most of the seating in the gate area was already taken when I arrived. The seats remaining were ignored by those already positioning for a traditional Ryanair stampede. Having carefully selected a seat, I waited and watched. At the first sign of movement, I sprang, slipping into the best possible position for anyone not paying extra, wearing a cast, or bearing a baby. Smooth as silk, without lying, shoving or elbowing, I exited the building second, but entered and exited the tarmac bus first. If Ryanair had not messed up their priority seating, I would have been first onto the plane after the cheaters. Still, I nabbed the very seat needed to ensure the seat beside me stayed empty, the only one on board.

Don't ask for that trick either. I swear nothing unfair, crude or cruel is involved.

My seat is also reportedly the safest.

--- + ---

Due to my seat choice, I also deplaned first at Shannon Airport, and with my Irish passport, reached the baggage carousel first. My bag appeared perfectly timed for snagging the bus to Ennis.

I do confess, I like traveling an econo-line economy class. I'm good at it. What I enjoyed more was arriving in Ireland. Though no one welcomes me, I feel the rush of homecoming. Is it the scent of the sea, or of the boggy ground? Maybe peat smoke perfuming the air, or just the atmospheric pressure comforts me. I don't know. I do know, deplaned, I am still flying, but I'm going nowhere now. I have come home.

--- + ---

What I did not enjoy, was finding that the first person met on Irish soil would be Nigerian. In Ennis, at any given moment, I might find myself surrounded by a dozen Nigerians or Congolese. Certainly the opposite combination is more usual, but that's nearly as bad. Are flocks of Shannon-siders settling on the banks of the Niger or Nile? No. Ireland did suffer most from emigration under capitalism; must we suffer most from immigration under capitalism? Go ahead, call me a racist now, since you have no other answer to the above questions, and Truth is a stranger to you.

If the destruction of culture and habitat in Africa and Asia due to globalization is evil out there, it's evil in Ireland too. I have traveled the world to view and appreciate other cultures and environments. I never stopped, never settled, never estranged someone else's home. I would not be permitted to stop. I would not be allowed to live elsewhere for free, or to work legally. Nor should I be. Why are people with no legal or moral right allowed to stop here?

In the capital of his home county, this Irish pilgrim could find no hostel bed. The "new" hostel had been commandeered for "refugees." One wouldn't mind for genuine refugees. These people patently have more money than I. From the parasitic class in their own countries, they fly here to exploit a society that gives free homes, cars and phones to them. At least the Germans who bought all our property, and the Poles who took all the jobs, had a legal right to do so. Other Eastern Europeans did not. Rumanian Gypsies have taken even the begging concession from native travelers.

I moved on, in wet and windy weather, into the countryside, looking for cheap accommodation. I succeeded in Kilkee, but lost my new umbrella on the bus. Chatting with the news agent nearest the bus stop, about my travels and travails, as you do in Ireland, I mentioned my mistake, when leaving. He followed me out, to offer a free umbrella, worth 20 euro. "Just pass it on," he insisted, "if you get your brelly back." My own was returned after one call to Bus Eireann, so I returned his—through a gale. Generous to a fault, Old Ireland is not dead, as long as that old shopkeeper lives.

=== + ===

For reading and contemplation while traveling the world, I appropriately brought with me *A 40-Day Journey in the Company of St. Francis*. As the book was loaned to me, to carry it proved comforting; reading it did not. Francis sure is a hard man for men being soft. I ain't arguing, I just guess I'm going to hell—not a comforting thought.

Yet, my tumultuous intestines have experienced a miraculous recovery regardless. I don't know if that's due to the healing grace of God conducted to me in an onion-domed chapel where believers pray for health, or, if the conduit is a candle lit in prayer for another's recovery. Maybe the wholesomeness of Polish food has restored me. Whatever the cause, God and my guts are granting me the respite needed to finish this book, and, just maybe, another journey.

CHAPTER 4

A Burst Appendix

7 November 08

Now that the election is over, I can admit being glad about Obama's comfortable win. Nice to see a black family in the White House. Nothing I ever expected to see. The Berlin Wall, the Iron Curtain, now this invisible curtain...we live in interesting times. Had Obama not won, and won convincingly, life in America, political and social, would have turned sour, even bloody.

Understand, I could never have voted for him, nor for Hillary. However, the first time I heard him address a crowd, back when Hillary remained presumptive president, I declared Obama the next prez of the USA. For, he addressed the very real fears of ordinary citizens, and looked as concerned as they did. He convincingly pledged to do something, something radically different. Even when Clinton and McCain closed in the polls, I never believed those results. As pollsters failed to phone cell phones, their efforts were worthless.

Believe me, I never believed Obama either. He never convinced *me* that he was the candidate for true honesty, change and hope. No-hoper Ron Paul was that. Everything Obama's opponents said about him is true. He's an old-fashioned Democrat populist pol in the pocket of anti-democratic special interests.

As evidenced in the Californian referendums, most Obama voters do not support the views of Obama backers. Barack won regardless because ordinary folks, betrayed by Republicans, grew desperate. In our "democracy," that's your choice: the lesser of two evils (or the evil of two lessers). Of course, we've yet to see if he is the lesser evil. The new messiah may indeed be the Anti-Christ.

=== + ===

That possibility renders interesting an admittedly unscientific poll taken during his campaign. My fellow travelers gave the following responses to this question: "If you were elected president, or dictator, what's the one thing you would want to see done, before being shot?"

The most popular reply, I'm proud to say, was my own original response. Near 20 percent promised free healthcare. More preventative care and mental treatment got specific mention. Healthcare is a right, or no one has rights. Nothing would do more to relieve undue stress on Americans, or to free up American industry, than universal healthcare. However, for the government to ensure the availability of affordable healthcare, does not require a takeover by a new bureaucracy.

The second choice was my second choice, though I swear I never suggested it: reform education. Introduce more accountability for teachers, more choice for parents, more cognitive thinking for pupils, this is the order of many "presidents," but not of Obama. Affordability of education to the third level, they also promised. Few were as radical as I, who would abolish the public school system, leaving only the obligation to finance every child's right to an education. A system of vouchers, not of propaganda, is what American citizens need. Some responders were merely reactionary, demanding that schools restore value-forming curriculums, apparently quite unaware that government involvement produces the opposite.

"Force responsibility back onto citizens, parents particularly," belongs maybe under *fix education*.

Not surprisingly, interest #3 picked up after the Market collapse. Ten percent of folks called for tighter regulation of the financial world, or the total restructuring of it. Even the elimination of private banking appealed to some dictators, doing away with the Federal Reserve, which sounds public but isn't.

The bureaucratic scamming and pyramid scheming of the insurance industry attracted the attention of the above financial reformers, as did Big Oil. Crowds with pitchforks, torches, tar and feathers searched for many CEOs.

Some respondents expressed more general concern for the economy. Wanting "to fix it," they pledged job creation, or job restoration to the USA. Others leaned dramatically left: "income equality; guaranteed housing; bailing out the foreclosed; breaking wild swings of capitalism; bringing back FDR; care for society's most vulnerable, the homeless and destitute; de-industrializing agri-business; unincorporating corporations." A few tilted right: "reform welfare; seal the borders; repeal NAFTA." Only one adamantly supported NAFTA. He'd met his wife in Canada due to the treaty, and honeymooned on the train. Ahhh…

One suggested the nationalization of only the Fortune 500 companies, to end most corruption at home and abroad.

Concern for the economy crossed into the next most popular reply: *end war,* specifically war in Iraq. The money is needed elsewhere: civilian research and development, or rebuilding infrastructure. The sole pro-war candidate spoke facetiously I trust. He intends to invade a small country, too small to fight back, ensuring his place in history, as a victorious war president.

Environmental concern also tended towards anti-war and pro-economy replies. Their war cry went "Alternative renewable energy!" Surprisingly, only one train rider promised to support public transport. What does that say? Only one would ban cars.

All folks promising government reform can't be lumped together as their views diverge so. One gent surprised me with his thoughtful answer. I nearly did not ask him at all, he looked so unresponsive. A tired businessman, maybe an insurance salesman, he demanded a Declaration of *Inter*dependence. Society should reward citizens according to how much of themselves they share with society. Exploitative and parasitic persons should be exploited by the people. Do whatever you like, but expect to be taxed or fined for selfish, irresponsible behavior. May God lighten the load of that weary man.

I didn't care for the tone of one woman who would restrict suffrage to citizens who aced tests in civics and logic. Another woman insisted the country should be run like a business, working with what works, not promises or dreams. Not only was her rhetoric Republican, she looked like Sarah Palin, and even had a son in Iraq. Her voice sounded better than Sarah's though. (Business can be run badly, evilly.)

Others, less elitist, called for power to the people. All power, political and economic, they would reduce to local, to restore community and family. Compulsory national service, both Left and Right seek. Destroying Left and Right in politics, or any party system, had very vocal advocates. Accountability, the ability to recall bad representatives immediately, some thought would suffice. One would ban all lobbying as bribery. Democratizing through the internet was put forward. Controlling the public payroll a few proposed, and one patriot promised if elected president to reduce his own pay to minimum wage.

Taken separately, tax-reformers formed the next largest, but very disparate group. Two decreed a balanced budget amendment; two sought flat tax. The latter hope to catch all who escape the tax net now: the very wealthy, tourists and aliens (from Mexico or the moon). Allocating your own taxes some advocated as a tool for democracy. Extra taxes on Republicans and assholes I heard would quickly make society more civil and solvent.

One notion pressed by three people would legalize drugs. A proselytizing tee-totaler, I favor this because history teaches that prohibition does not work, is in fact counterproductive, and does corrupt all.

Another three, already corrupted, made me re-word my question more carefully. All guys, one proposed sex with all women; one only wanted two at the same time; one would be satisfied with one, i.e., Sarah Palin.

All other answers singled only. Some individuals just can't let go of a pet peeve. Particularly petty dictators would mandate: opening Area 51; vegetarianism; veganism; banning rap music; banning thongs or spandex on fatties. One woman still pushes for equal pay for women. Doubly surprising, only one young man would ironclad the right to choose abortion. He loathes the religious right. No one suggested overturning Roe v. Wade as their priority.

Presumably an Obama supporter, one optimist claimed he would end all racial tension. Possibly an Obama opponent, one cynic plans to reform the slobbering media, restricting ownership.

My favorite answers were not from me, or from the persons who provided them. Kurt Vonnegut's idea on welfare reform appeared: *no welfare check is issued until a book report has been submitted.* William F. Buckley, a conservative mayoral candidate in N.Y.C., when asked for his first act if elected, replied, "Demand a recount." That reminds how one young lady, who looked radiant but not too bright, proved my impression wrong. When asked, "What would you do if elected president?" she quipped, "Leave the country."

Finally, I'd like to cheat, to change my answer after hearing all the others, because no one else promised this. As dictator, I would surrender all power after establishing (for the first time in America) democracy. Now that we see where betraying our one ideal has brought us, shouldn't we try government of the people, by the people, for the people?